EMBRACE
FOR
IMPACT!

EMBRACE FOR IMPACT!

Crack the MyOS Code.
Win the Inner War.

JOHN FAIRCLOUGH

WREN HOUSE
press

COPYRIGHT © 2026 JOHN FAIRCLOUGH
All rights reserved.

EMBRACE FOR IMPACT!
Crack the MyOS Code. Win the Inner War.
First Edition

ISBN	978-1-967115-22-8	Hardcover
	978-1-967115-21-1	Paperback
	978-1-967115-20-4	Ebook
	978-1-967115-23-5	Audiobook

LCCN 2025927238

To Bean, VV, Rozie, and Johnny.
Even saying your names makes me smile.

And to everyone who helped me or trusted me to help them, thank you.

CONTENTS

Introduction: Be You! xi

PART 1. THE 8 PARADOXES OF LEADERSHIP

Paradox 1: Perfection Is Flawed 3
Paradox 2: Boundaries Build Bridges 19
Paradox 3: Clarity Is Complicated 37
Paradox 4: Failure Fuels Success 57
Paradox 5: Accountability Creates Freedom 71
Paradox 6: Power Grows When It's Given Away 93
Paradox 7: Vulnerabilities Are Your Superpowers 107
Paradox 8: Your Right Answers Are Different Than Mine 123
Wrap-Up 133

PART 2. THE BE YOU! MANIFESTO™

Overview 139
Worksheets 145
Worksheet 1: Defining Your Core Values and Core Virtues 147

Worksheet 2: Personality Insights   153
Worksheet 3: Develop Your Definition of
   a Good Person   158
Worksheet 4: Standard Boundaries   161
Worksheet 5: Insights from Others   164
Worksheet 6: Your Priorities   168
Worksheet 7: My Resilience Reminders   170
Worksheet 8: My Words of Encouragement   173
Wrap-Up: The Manifesto That Will Change
   Everything   175

PART 3. ACT & RECOVER TOOLKIT™

Overview   181
Act Tool: Activating MyOS™   185
Act Tool: FOCUS   195
Act Tool: Share Your Gratitude   201
Act Tool: Manifesto Lite (Warning Label)   209
Recover Tool: RESTORE   213
Recover Tool: Optimization Mindset   219
Recover Tool: A Personal Board of Advisors   227
Recover Tool: The BUILD Method   235

Conclusion   243
About the Author   247

INTRODUCTION

BE YOU!

The Best Advice I Ever Gave Myself

There's a mantra I live by: Our toughest challenges are the moments God uses to introduce us to ourselves.

My formative years were a study in these moments. Growing up in extreme poverty, I bounced between other people's houses from the seventh grade on—learning to "go along to get along." (Maybe that's why now I'd rather live in squalor than in a place that didn't feel like mine.) Regardless, I never really had a home, which was confirmed in my late teens during one of those tough moments—a pivotal moment that, to be honest, I never saw coming.

I had recently moved in with an older cousin whom I admire deeply. He lived in Florida, and when he invited me to stay with him, I jumped at the chance. Around him,

I felt strong and protected. I knew he loved me. But after a while, I had to face the reality that Florida wasn't where I belonged. The life was too fast, not what I wanted. So I made the tough decision to go back "home" (where I had been staying before leaving for Florida) and get my life on the right track.

Except that wasn't what happened. When I knocked on the door of the house where I'd been living, the people I was staying with—family members, no less—looked at me and said I couldn't come back in.

"But I have no place to live."

"Too bad," they said. "You should've thought about that before you left for Florida."

I remember standing there, backpack in hand, the words "too bad" echoing in my head. I'd just left a place that didn't fit me and came back ready to start over, only to find the door to the life I hoped to start slammed shut in my face. It was a devastating blow...and in fact, that rejection changed me in ways that still affect me today.

I had come back with the intention of getting myself together, but in that instant, my priority changed to stabilizing myself. I did things I'm not proud of to scrape together enough money to buy an old car I ended up living in. For six months, I parked on crowded suburban streets, hoping to blend in. I kept my clothes in the trunk, joined a health club just so I'd have a place to shower, and every night I crawled under a blanket in that back seat, eyes wide open, listening to fights and arguments echo down the block.

I was scared, but I wasn't going to run. I'd lie there completely still until a strange calmness settled in. Over and over, I'd whisper to myself, "Everything will be okay," then close my eyes.

Different family members asked me later why I didn't move in with them. But what we're fighting on the inside often looks so different from what others see. I had resolved that I was never going to rely on other people again. And no wonder: I was tired of being let down. Tired of waiting for someone to save me, especially begrudgingly.

God introduced me to myself that day, and what I learned was something very simple: I needed to forge my own way.

Maybe you've never been in this exact situation—kicked out of your house, forced to live in your car—but I bet you've felt like you've had doors slammed shut on you that should have been kept open. I bet, since you're reading this book, that you're searching for your own answers. For ways to overcome the obstacles before you.

Your challenges might be personal. They might be professional. They might have occurred years ago, or they might be happening right now. Honestly, it doesn't really matter. God is introducing you to yourself, just like He did for me at that moment.

I wouldn't change what happened to me for the world. Yes, the road was bumpy, but I slayed that dragon. In doing so, I learned something about myself: I'm not the victim of other people's decisions. I'm in control of what I do. I'm grateful for the rejection. It created the situation that sparked my *real* introduction to John—the version who is no longer the victim of circumstance. It helped me become the man and the leader I am today.

It did something else too: It made me ask a vital question, one that I hope you will ask yourself as you read through this book. *What if the key to becoming an extraordinary leader wasn't about learning more, doing more, or following someone else's playbook?*

What if the most powerful thing you could do was trust and amplify the person you already are? Most leadership and self-help books tell you to fix yourself—to push harder, change more, follow the steps of those who "made it." But that's the problem. The more you try to force yourself into someone else's mold, the further you drift from your greatest strength—your authenticity. That's where MyOS™—your Operating System for Becoming Psychologically Indestructible—comes in. It's a system that lets you cut through the noise and lead (and live) as your true self.

THE BATTLE NO ONE TALKS ABOUT

While so much of this book can be applied to personal challenges, MyOS™ is especially helpful in becoming an extraordinary leader. That's because the hardest battle in leadership isn't external. The problem isn't about making tough decisions or managing teams. The most difficult struggle is truly internal—facing the pressure to conform. Fighting the fear of judgment. Handling the quiet self-doubt that whispers: *Am I doing this right? Am I enough?*

There were times I betrayed what felt natural and got exactly what I was chasing, and other times when I stood fully aligned with who I am and watched everything fall apart. That kind of whiplash doesn't just mess with your head. It makes you question if you're any good at all.

If you've ever experienced this—ever felt as if you're an imposter, as if you've been forced to "fake it until you make it"—if you've silenced yourself to fit in or second-guessed your instincts because they didn't match the conventional playbook, then this book is for you.

I believe the root cause of so much anxiety is when people are not being themselves. Every person can stand tall when their decisions align with who they are. But whenever we shape ourselves to meet expectations that don't fit our authentic selves—when we chase others' definitions of success, when we silence our instincts to avoid judgment—doubt creeps in and anxiety takes hold. I know this firsthand. Between enduring extreme poverty, never having a stable home as a child (I transferred schools more times than any kid should), and being surrounded by people battling their own mental health struggles, I had every reason to doubt myself. If I were wired differently, I'm sure debilitating anxiety would have found a home with me. But instead, the turmoil I was in snuck up in other ways. I became hyper-vigilant, which meant I overcorrected when I started to fall out of alignment with who I was. That wasn't healthy either: I tolerated a lot of garbage because I wanted to maintain my control of self.

The problems bled into my professional life. For years, I led the way I thought I was supposed to—following the playbook, doing what was expected. But no matter how much I tried, something always felt off. I was working harder than ever, losing myself in the process. It wasn't until I let go of the need to do it "right" and started trusting myself that everything changed.

I now know that the best leaders—the ones who make an impact, who create real change—aren't the ones who blend in. They're the ones who embrace who they are in all their individuality.

It took me a long time to understand this. I got so caught up in the mission and chasing results that I lost sight of myself. When I started to embrace who I was, though, I discovered that what I really love, more than scaling and growth and revenue, is trust. I love authenticity. Those matter more to me than the incomplete lens of financial performance.

INTRODUCTION ✦ XVII

I love being the kind of leader that people can count on—the kind of leader who is bold enough to be themself. These are the ones who make a real impact in people's lives and in organizations. They create lasting change and genuine inspiration. They embrace who they are. The most effective leaders are the ones who stop playing the "fit-in" game and start being themselves. But since most of us have been playing the game for so long, we need to stop and get to know ourselves again.

I know that this can seem easier said than done, so later in the book, I've laid out a series of lessons and exercises to help you do a personal deep dive that will help you rediscover many special things about yourself, the traits those around you need to see: the unique parts of who you are that will equip you to be a better leader (or even a better spouse and/or parent).

This book will also help you set boundaries that show others what to expect from you and remind you what to expect from yourself. The way people set boundaries in leadership mirrors how they set boundaries in their personal lives. This book teaches frameworks that improve both.

This book will show you how to lead with clarity and confidence, without second-guessing yourself. It will help you break free from fear, self-doubt, and the need to please others. More importantly, it will offer new ways to view challenges and learn to forgive yourself, turning "failures" into fuel for growth. In the end, you'll have everything you need to make better decisions, build stronger relationships, and align your life with your true priorities.

Ultimately, it will help you be you—not just at work, but in every part of your life.

HOW MyOS™ WORKS

MyOS™ unfolds in three parts to forge your indestructible self:

- **The 8 Paradoxes of Leadership**: These counterintuitive truths will expand how you think about yourself, situations, and people.

- **The Be You! Manifesto™**: Here you will find worksheets that will help you define and share exactly who you are and how you operate.

- **The Act & Recover Toolkit™**: This will give you simple, repeatable strategies you can use to put these insights into action every day.

Here's how it all breaks down and forms the MyOS™ Framework:

The 8 Paradoxes of Leadership	1. Perfection Is Flawed 2. Boundaries Build Bridges 3. Clarity Is Complicated 4. Failure Fuels Success 5. Accountability Creates Freedom 6. Power Grows When It's Given Away 7. Vulnerabilities Are Your Superpowers 8. Your Right Answers Are Different Than Mine
The Be You! Manifesto™	Visit *www.johnfairclough.com/book-resources* to view a sample of my personal Be You! Manifesto™
The Act & Recover Toolkit™	MyOS™ Weekly 1-on-1 • **FOCUS**: Your Difficult Decision Framework • **Share Your Gratitude**: Rewire Your Mind, Transform Your World • **Manifesto Lite** (Warning Label) • **RESTORE**: The MyOS™ Trust & Apology Framework • Optimization Mindset • A Personal Board of Advisors • **The BUILD Method**: Navigate Difficult Conversations

Together, these three parts comprise the MyOS™ Framework.

THE EIGHT PARADOXICAL TRUTHS THAT UNLOCK AUTHENTIC LEADERSHIP

I didn't have a road map for building a company, leading teams, or making high-stakes decisions. No one sat me down and taught me how to lead. There was no blueprint—just me, figuring it out in real time, making mistakes, and learning the hard way.

I fought battles that most people never saw: the ones in my business, the ones in my bank account, and the ones in my own head. I wasn't just trying to succeed—I was trying to survive. Countless times I didn't even have a single dollar to pay my bills. Somehow, I never missed payroll for my team. I went a long time without getting paid and ate plenty of tomato-and-cracker sandwiches. I didn't have the luxury of quitting. I just couldn't live broke anymore.

I was drowning. I did everything the so-called experts said to do, but nothing seemed to work, at least not consistently. I read the books. I studied the strategies. I tried to follow the formulas for success. But instead of feeling stronger, I felt drained. I had no gas in the tank, but the job still needed to get done. So, I dug deeper. I found something inside me—something that refused to let me stop. I coined the phrase, "If my life depended on it, I'm going to live," because I had no other choice. If it was crucial, I wasn't going to fail. I acted like my life was on the line. In many ways, it was. At the very least, my financial life was.

I've always been skeptical of authority. (Bear in mind, "authority" and "expert" are not the same thing. Authority is tied to the power that people have, while expertise is tied to knowledge. When I listen to experts, whether I choose to apply what they're saying or not comes down to their subject matter and my belief in what they are saying. I have no issue with that. It's the person in power who oppresses or who does not handle what is in their care well that I have disdain for.) Some of that was instilled in me by my grandmother and her sons. The rest I learned firsthand—watching people in power make the wrong calls, let people down, or prove that they didn't have the answers they claimed to have.

The result of this innate disdain: I learned to rely on me. John bets on John.

As part of that journey, I came to understand eight paradoxes—counterintuitive truths that, when embraced, shatter limiting beliefs, eliminate the anxiety that holds us back, and elevate how we lead and live. These are the paradoxes that this book is structured around, and every one of them is something I had to learn the hard way. I had to unlearn what I thought was right, break through old mental patterns, and replace them with deeper truths that actually worked.

These paradoxes weren't just leadership principles—they were survival tactics. They kept me in the fight when everything else told me to quit. Eventually, they became more than just ways to survive; they became the foundation for unshakable resilience and the confidence to lead as myself.

They changed everything for me. And if you let them, they'll change everything for you too. We'll go deep into the paradoxes in the upcoming section, but here is a brief breakdown of each of them so you can start to get them into your head (and your heart):

1. **Perfection Is Flawed**: The endless chase for perfection isn't making you stronger; it's suffocating your confidence and slowing you down. The leaders who thrive aren't the ones who get everything right, but the ones who embrace their imperfections, adapt quickly, and recognize the strengths in others. Trying to be perfect all the time doesn't make you a better leader; it makes you hesitant, fearful, and disconnected.

2. **Boundaries Build Bridges**: Saying yes to everything and everyone doesn't make you more effective—it drains your energy and builds frustration. The strongest leaders protect their time and focus, knowing that clear boundaries don't push people away; they pull the right people closer.

3. **Clarity Is Complicated**: Clarity isn't about having all the answers; it's about knowing who you are, where you stand, and where you're trying to go. The best leaders take action with what they

have, making decisions they can be proud of and adjusting along the way.

4. **Failure Fuels Success**: Failure isn't a detour; it's an essential part of the path. The strongest leaders embrace their failures, gaining lifelong insights that sharpen their instincts, resilience, and impact far beyond the moment. Setbacks can be the best training grounds.

5. **Accountability Creates Freedom**: Accountability isn't a cage—it's the key to real freedom. Leaders who take ownership of their actions gain trust, clarity, and control over their success, while those who avoid responsibility stay stuck in chaos, uncertainty, and frustration. Rules don't limit freedom; they create it.

6. **Power Grows When It's Given Away**: The tighter you grip control, the weaker your leadership becomes. True power impacts people even when you're not in the room. Trust, empowerment, and elevating others are the keys here. Lift others up, and you'll see how powerful you are.

7. **Vulnerabilities Are Your Superpowers**: Vulnerability isn't a weakness; it's what makes

leadership real. The strongest leaders use vulnerability to build connection. They balance openness with wisdom. Hiding your struggles doesn't make you strong; it doesn't even make you look less weak. It makes you look fake.

8. **Your Right Answers Are Different Than Mine**: Success isn't found in someone else's playbook; it's built by trusting your own. The strongest leaders don't seek validation in someone else's path. They define success on their terms, aligning their decisions with their values, strengths, and vision.

Embracing these paradoxes gave me the confidence to be myself, stripping away years of frustration over why things weren't working. When I embraced these eight truths, I realized that I had wasted too much time chasing other people's clichés. My real success came when I stopped searching for the right answers and started trusting my own.

THE ELEMENTS OF LEADERSHIP: SEPARATE BUT CONNECTED

The paradoxes help you expand how you think about leadership. They stretch your perspective and build your awareness. But leadership is not just something you understand. It is something you practice. Situations in leadership are where those inner tensions come to life. They are the everyday arenas where mindset becomes action and where theory is tested by reality.

- **Leading Yourself**: Everything starts here. If you don't lead yourself with clarity, resilience, and authenticity, you can't lead anyone else effectively.

- **Leading Another**: Leadership happens in relationships. The best leaders don't control. They empower.

- **Leading Teams**: Bringing out the best in people, aligning different strengths toward a shared vision.

- **Leading Organizations**: At this level, leadership is about culture, vision, and legacy.

- **Being Led**: The best leaders know how to follow, listen, and learn.

- **Influencing Without Authority**: Leadership isn't about a position; it's about impact.

Each of these elements is separate but deeply connected. The way you lead yourself affects how you lead others. The trust you build in relationships shapes your team culture. And the humility you show as a follower makes you a better leader.

THE BE YOU! MANIFESTO™

The paradoxes, not to mention the elements of leadership, are crucial to understand if you want to be an extraordinary leader, but they aren't the whole story. I wasted years exhausted by expectations that weren't mine, saying yes when I wanted to say no, and trying to be "good" in everyone else's eyes. I thought if I just worked harder, people would understand me, respect me, stop questioning me. I was self-erasing. But the harder I tried to fit their mold, the more miserable I became. That's not leadership; that's performance.

I didn't need another leadership book. I needed a framework that would help me remember who I really was when the world tried to make me forget. That's what the Be You! Manifesto™ is: not another formula to cram yourself into, but a reminder to trust and amplify the person you already are.

This Manifesto is simple but not easy. It helps you define your core identity, set the boundaries that keep you sane, and protect the energy that keeps you in the fight. It's not about perfection. It's about alignment. And when you lead from that place, you become a powerful force.

The Be You! Manifesto™ didn't make me perfect. It made me real. That's the only kind of leader worth following, and the only one you'll ever need to be.

THE ACT & RECOVER TOOLKIT™

With the Manifesto, I was in charge but not in control—stretched thin by chaos, weak boundaries, and no clear sense of where I ended and everyone else began. I'd get up every day determined to do right by people, only to feel drained by them.

I built this Toolkit because self-awareness alone doesn't change your life. Action does. The Be You! Manifesto™ reveals who you are. The Toolkit makes sure you live it—especially when life tests you.

This Toolkit is simple, but it's not soft. It helps you align your choices with who you really are, handle hard conversations without apology, and manage your energy so you don't burn out doing work that doesn't matter. It's not a motivational poster—it's a set of tools that keep you steady in the messiest moments of leadership and life.

If you're ready to stop reacting and start leading on your terms, this is where that begins. The Act & Recover Toolkit™ doesn't give you a new mask to wear—it hands you back the keys to your real self.

A LEADERSHIP JOURNEY THAT NEVER ENDS

I hope you see by now that this book isn't about checking a box or following a formula. It's about developing a way of leading and a way of living that keeps you aligned, confident, and growing. It's about building your own MyOS™ that helps you stay true to yourself—no matter what pressures, challenges, or expectations come your way. It's about leading in a way that reflects your unique strengths, values, and vision. And most importantly, it's about giving you permission to lead *your* way.

Remember, God introduces us to ourselves through our toughest challenges. These difficult intersections pave the way for who we become. MyOS™ turns those moments into the strength that drives us forward.

Look, you don't need yet another strategy. You don't need to become someone else. You need the clarity, courage, and habits to be who you are and a way to share this clearly with those closest to you. This book will help you self-coach and scale your impact without burnout.

Let's begin.

THE 8 PARADOXES OF LEADERSHIP

1: Perfection Is Flawed
2: Boundaries Build Relationships
3: Clarity Is Complicated
4: Failure Fuels Success
5: Accountability Creates Freedom
6: Power Grows When It's Given Away
7: Vulnerabilities Are Your Superpowers
8: Your Right Answers Are Different Than Mine

PARADOX 1

PERFECTION IS FLAWED

So many of us are exhausted from trying to get everything right. No matter how much effort we put in, it never feels like enough. We hesitate, overthink, and delay action because we're afraid of falling short. Though perfectionism sounds noble, it isn't. It slowly crushes your confidence and joy.

While striving for excellence has its place, relying on perfection for approval or happiness isn't just unnecessary—it's harmful to your growth, confidence, and well-being. In this paradox, we will explore how perfectionism often limits you. You'll learn to identify situations in which the pursuit of perfection becomes a trap that hinders creativity, progress, and connection within your team.

By embracing imperfection—which can be a gateway to connection—you will unlock the power of resilience, trust, and authenticity in your leadership style. You'll also discover how embracing your own flaws and those of others can foster deeper relationships and create a more supportive, high-performing team.

My hope is that, as you embrace imperfection, you'll also begin to recognize your own worth beyond performance or approval. True leadership isn't about projecting a flawless image; it's about showing up authentically, building trust, and empowering others to do the same. Growth, connection, and success come not through perfection, but through resilience, humility, and the courage to lead as your real self. The truth is, nobody's impressed by your perfection anyway. They're moved by your scars, your comebacks, and your willingness to keep showing up when it's hard.

This paradox challenges you to move beyond the need for flawless execution and focus instead on the real drivers of success. You'll walk away with practical tools to free yourself from the weight of perfectionism and lead with greater authenticity and impact.

Don't get me wrong: Perfectionism is not inherently bad and can drive excellence when kept in balance. But when it becomes the standard for self-worth, it becomes a heavy burden. As you'll see, it's progress, not perfection, that builds confidence, trust, and lasting success.

1.1. REAL, NOT PERFECT

Getting divorced created some of the saddest conversations I've ever had to have. Divorce causes so much pain. I don't know when the world became so numb to it, but it has. But it nearly broke me, especially when I saw how sad my children were about my wife and me separating. Even now, just thinking about it can make me well up. I knew my kids didn't want to pick sides—but I also knew they felt pulled to. Going through that felt like a vicious cycle, especially because I have vivid memories of various family members talking badly about my dad. And even though he wasn't really there for me, I didn't want to believe he was garbage like they said. I wanted to think my dad was good, because that meant I came from good.

I never forgot that. So when my kids were hurting, I worked hard to make sure they knew the truth: Their mom was a good woman and a good mom, and she loved them very much. No matter how sad or angry I was, I didn't want to pass that pain to them. They deserved to hold on to what was good, even in something as imperfect as divorce.

That experience taught me that imperfection doesn't break you—pretending it's not there does. Sometimes the strongest thing you can do for the people you love is let them see the cracks and protect what's worth protecting inside them.

I had to come to terms with the fact that the ideal upbringing I wanted so desperately to provide was gone. Now more than ever, my children needed a real dad—not a perfect one.

You might never have gone through a divorce, but the lesson applies nevertheless: Imperfection isn't a flaw. But if you try to cover it up, you fail to be the kind of person *and* the kind of leader the people around you need. Focus on being real, not perfect, and you'll have a more peaceful journey.

1.2. THE PRODIGAL SON AND IMPERFECTION

I have a friend who struggled with the weight of imperfection in a way that deeply moved me. She grew up with a terrible relationship with her father, was caught up in drugs, alcohol, and promiscuity, and found herself in a destructive cycle. At first glance, you would never know she had gone through so many hard things—she is beautiful, is funny, and has been put on a pedestal by so many. But as we got to know each other, it was clear to me that there was a lot going on under the surface. One day, I commented on her depth and started asking her questions to get to the heart of *her*, and she let her whole story out. Somehow she knew she could trust me. Perhaps it's not surprising: We had the kind of friendship where we didn't talk every day, but we were there for each other. I knew she saw me as a helpful person if she started to slip. When she was strong, she knew she had my support; when she was weak, she could call on that support. I was the reminder of her value when she needed it most.

Talking to her that day, I was shocked by her story. Crucially, though, I didn't feel pity or judgment. Instead, I felt compassion and a deep understanding of her pain. After she finished, she looked at me, perhaps wondering if I was going to judge her. Immediately, I jumped in and told her, "It sucks that you went through all that, but it's pretty cool that you had such a powerful experience. Look how far you've come." She was taken aback, confused by how I could see her struggle in such a positive light. So, I shared a story with her, the one that has always helped me understand the beauty in imperfection.

I asked her if she knew the biblical story of the Prodigal Son. She didn't, so I gave her a brief overview: The wayward son returns home after squandering his inheritance, and his father forgives him completely, offering him unconditional love and acceptance. The real kicker, I told her, is the older brother—resentful of the younger brother's return, believing he had earned his place and the father's love through hard work and loyalty. In contrast, the father's love for the son who "failed" is so profound that he throws a feast for him. This is a love that sees the person, not their mistakes.

I explained that forgiveness is not just about letting go of a wrong—it's about saying, "You are worth more than how your actions made me feel." It's the act of looking beyond imperfection and embracing someone for who they truly are. I shared some of my own embarrassing moments, times I made mistakes and learned from them, to show her that imperfection was something we all share and something that can be the foundation for a deeper connection.

The Prodigal Son's return isn't just about him coming back to his father. It's about a father's love that welcomes the broken, the lost, and the imperfect. And in embracing that imperfection, we all have the potential to grow, learn, and transform.

Without grace for imperfection, people stay stuck. Feeling ashamed, isolated, and afraid to grow is a terrible way to live. As leaders, we need to help people see their worth even when they're at their worst. That's what gives them the courage to rise.

I could see that my words helped her. Though it looks like she was the one receiving the help, I felt good on the inside because I was making a difference in someone's life. Had everything been perfect in her life, both of us would have missed out on this opportunity to reframe imperfection into something positive.

1.3. EMBRACE IMPERFECTION TO UNLOCK POTENTIAL

Perfectionism can often seem like a noble pursuit, driving us to achieve excellence and high standards. However, it can also become a trap that holds us back from growth. When we place too much value on being flawless, we may carry a heavy burden, feeling unworthy whenever we fall short. When taken too far, perfectionism can prevent us from embracing progress, learning from mistakes, and creating meaningful connections. The key is to find balance—to strive for quality while recognizing that growth often comes through imperfection.

Leadership often begins with the illusion that perfection is the ultimate goal. Many leaders believe they must present a flawless image to inspire confidence in their teams, clients, or stakeholders. Yet this pursuit of perfection often becomes a trap, leading to stress, inefficiency, and strained relationships. The truth is that embracing imperfection allows leaders to focus on what truly matters: prioritizing effectively, fostering trust, and creating an environment in which both they and their teams can thrive.

Think about the process of getting ready for a big event. A woman might try on five different outfits, send photos to her best friend for feedback, and agonize over whether her shoes perfectly match her dress. It's not just about being "ready"; it's about feeling confident. For some, their confidence comes only when everything is "just right." But is this really necessary? Imagine the stress and energy spent—and how much easier it would be to embrace the imperfections and simply enjoy the evening. Leadership is no different. The pressure to present a perfect image can be exhausting, and it's often unnecessary.

Now let's consider a professional scenario. I once worked with a team member who was a perfectionist to the core. We often argued about strategy because he insisted that every job had to meet his high standards of excellence. What he didn't realize (and he's far from alone in this) is that standards without context can quickly turn into unnecessary—and sometimes inappropriate—expenses. It came to a head when we broke down the steps he believed were required to complete a certain job "with excellence." When we did the math, his approach would have taken 2.5 times longer and cost more than two times what the client was willing to spend. "Is a solution the client can't afford really a solution at all?" I asked him.

This experience highlighted a critical truth: Without refinement, many so-called "ideals" are completely impractical.

Another powerful example came from a vendor evaluating a storefront repair. The client's lease was expiring in twelve months, so they really needed an affordable solution to cover that. The vendor insisted, "This needs to be replaced. I only do the job right, or I don't do it at all." His words seemed noble—a professional committed to quality. But he missed the most fundamental component of success: It's not about the theoretical best solution—it's about what the buyer actually needs and values. In this case, the $35,000 replacement was out of the question when a $3,500 repair met the client's needs perfectly. This insight became a cornerstone of what I taught my team: Define success by the customer's needs and objectives, not by arbitrary standards of excellence.

Through experiences like these, I came to understand that imperfection isn't a limitation; it's an invitation. It invites creativity, collaboration, and trust. By letting go of the need to control every detail, I created space for my team to take ownership of their work. They solved problems, brought forward ideas, and grew into leaders themselves. And in doing so, they taught me that imperfection is the foundation of progress. It's the cornerstone that will allow you to create environments in which others can solve, build, and grow.

1.4. RECOGNIZE THAT YOU MATTER

Good leadership inspires hope, always. This cannot be overstated. Hope flows from leaders who know their own value—but without it, everything they try to build eventually crumbles. That's because self-worth is the foundation of effective leadership. If you don't recognize your value, it becomes nearly impossible to inspire confidence in others.

People chase perfection because they secretly believe they're not enough. This is key. The stronger your sense of self-worth, the less you feel the need to prove you're flawless. When you know you matter, you stop trying to be perfect and start focusing on what really counts: setting clear boundaries, making honest decisions, and showing up real. Put another way, perfectionism isn't just about looking flawless—it's about believing you don't already have what you need.

I think one of the reasons this shows up is because so many entrepreneurs chase more and more insights before they have even processed what they have already learned. When I'm coaching someone, I often encourage them to stop trying to learn more and spend some time processing what they have already experienced. It's amazing how much we already know. For example, think about the last time or two when you felt like you were the victim. Examine that situation to find a relevant, usable lesson—and not the false ones like "I learned to not trust people." I mean meaningful lessons. Said differently, if I were to watch the tape of your life, I am sure I would find a bunch of situations that you see as ugly challenges and I see as incredible opportunities. Learning to see things through that lens is key to developing your self-worth and becoming an extraordinary leader.

It really can be that simple (not easy, but simple), but for many leaders, the journey to self-worth is anything but straightforward. It often begins with deeply ingrained patterns of undervaluing oneself, shaped by personal experiences, and evolves through moments of clarity, boundary-setting, and a commitment to authenticity.

Growing up in other people's homes, I learned to prioritize others' feelings over my own to avoid conflict. It became second nature to fade into the background, suppressing my needs and emotions. Over time, I internalized a belief that my feelings didn't matter because I am strong enough to endure and overcome them. This pattern followed me into adulthood, shaping my relationships and decisions. I'd go out of my way to accommodate others, often at the expense of my own well-being.

One moment marked a turning point. A family member had come to rely on me emotionally and financially, to the point where their expectations felt suffocating. Eventually, I had to do something. I remember telling them, "I'm not your husband. I didn't sign up to hear your daily drama." Saying those words felt both harsh and liberating. For the first time, I asserted my value and set a boundary. I recognized that my needs and priorities mattered too.

At that moment, I realized I was changing. I started pulling back on being that person's crutch, preserving more energy and time for my children and other things that matter to me. But asserting my value didn't come without consequences. Suddenly the very people I was giving so much to turned to gossiping against me. My closest friend was laughing about it, then said bluntly, "John, you know what? It's your fault. You make them think they're you. They act strong, but without you their lives would really suck."

I did not like hearing those words, but in a lot of ways he was right. These relationships were built on their dependence on me. When I withheld my support, they turned on me. Suddenly I was not the person that had supported them for years; I was a jerk who was making their lives worse. My cousin captured it best when he'd say "Anchors away" each time I walked away from these dynamics.

This realization extended to my professional life. I tolerated a lot of wrong things that were not good for me or the business. As I started to apply this paradox to my life, though, I started looking for ways to address those things. Recognizing my value and position, I determined that I was not going to be stopped—I was going to build the life and business that I wanted. My life was like a gear in a watch, and now that I wanted to turn differently, a bunch of other gears that connected to me were going to have to change to work with me again. Some relationships, both personal and professional, fell apart as I made this shift. It was painful but necessary.

Despite the pain, I noticed how much more present I became when I made and set boundaries. Funny enough, my peace grew as I spent more time on the things I wanted to. I felt freedom from certain things, and freedom to do things *I* wanted to do.

The lesson here: Leadership, I've learned, is about embracing your unique strengths and playing your own game. My plays are designed around me, and no one else can run them quite like I can. Recognizing this allowed me to stop comparing myself to others and focus on building relationships and teams that deserved to be part of my life.

1.5. LEAD THROUGH AUTHENTICITY

Authentic leadership begins with accepting that you don't need to be perfect or have all the answers. None of us are perfect, but we can make our next decision the best one we know how. Embracing imperfection isn't just freeing—it's necessary to create the humility needed for calmer decisions. Authenticity builds trust, and trust is the foundation of every meaningful relationship, both personal and professional. To lead through authenticity is to be true to yourself, align your actions with your values, and inspire others to do the same.

How does this apply to you? Simple: When you see your own worth, you model confidence for your teams, creating a ripple effect of trust and empowerment. You are better situated to be followed. You let go quickly, forgive easily, and roll with the punches.

Authenticity starts with understanding what truly defines your leadership values. For me, this realization came through the process of uncovering my company's core values. I didn't hand the task to a marketing team or borrow someone else's ideas. Instead, I sat down and made two lists: one of all the things I loved about how people behaved, and another of the things I couldn't stand. Then, I crumpled up the list of things I loved and focused on the opposite of what I hated. What emerged was a deeply personal set of values that reflected not only what I wanted from my team, but also how I aspired to lead.

For instance, "Honor the Promise" was one of my core values. At first pass, it looks simple, like keeping your word. But the deeper (and uncommon) sense of it lies in keeping the implied promise. I ask people we hire, "Why are you here?" They almost always have a difficult time answering the question. So I tell them, "You're here to make us a better, stronger company. Otherwise, why would we hire you?"

It's the same for relationships: The promise isn't just about commitment; it's about being fully present, fully invested, and making others feel wanted and valued. That's what "Honor the Promise" means to me—it's about going beyond the surface and fulfilling the deeper expectation of trust and reliability.

Defining core values is a deeply personal exercise. When done honestly it becomes a mirror, not a marketing slogan. It is one more reason authenticity is not just helpful in leadership; it is essential. Ultimately, leading through authenticity means rejecting the temptation to emulate someone else's leadership style and instead embracing your own unique path. As we'll explore in paradox 8, your right answers are different from mine, and that's what makes leadership a deeply personal journey. By showing up as your true self—flaws, strengths, and all—you give others permission to do the same. This is how trust is built, how teams transform, and how leadership becomes something far greater than simply hitting targets.

> **TAKEAWAYS**
>
> Embracing imperfection isn't about lowering standards; it's about recognizing that growth comes from willingness to adapt, learn, and move forward. Perfectionism often paralyzes leaders, locking them into a fear of failure and a need for control that stifles creativity and progress. By shifting the focus from being flawless to being effective, leaders not only free themselves from the impossible burden of perfection but also create an environment in which their teams feel empowered to take risks and grow. This approach fosters resilience, trust, and collaboration—qualities that are far more valuable than any illusion of perfection.
>
> As leaders, our most profound impact lies not in being flawless but in being authentic, approachable, and human. When we embrace our imperfections and model humility, we inspire others to do the same.

Imperfections are not weaknesses; they are opportunities to connect, learn, and build something extraordinary. By prioritizing progress over perfection and authenticity over appearances, you can transform your leadership, deepening relationships and paving the way for meaningful, sustainable success.

You don't have to carry the exhausting weight of perfection any longer. The freedom to lead, connect, and create impact comes not from proving you're flawless, but from embracing the real, evolving, and imperfect version of yourself.

PARADOX 2

BOUNDARIES BUILD BRIDGES

Learning to embrace imperfection is a big step toward becoming an extraordinary leader, but at the end of the day, wouldn't it be great to have peace? The kind of peace where you can be yourself and behave according to your personal definition of a good leader? Well, the key to that is boundaries.

Boundaries are not barriers—they are bridges that connect you to what matters most. Setting them is like a present from you to you, that everyone gets to enjoy.

Too often peace feels out of reach. You stretch yourself thin trying to meet everyone's expectations, saying yes when you should say no, until you're left handling everything except what actually matters most to you.

Leadership often carries the misconception that true connection comes from being endlessly available and accommodating, but this mindset leads to burnout, missed opportunities, and strained relationships, even at home. A leader consumed with low-impact tasks will eventually fail to seize transformative moments because their energy and focus are misaligned.

To overcome that, I invite you to learn to see boundaries as acts of respect for yourself and others instead of as dividing walls. They empower leaders to build connections based on honesty, clarity, and shared commitment. And when your team honors your boundaries, celebrate their effort. Let them see the empowerment that clear limits bring, modeling the behavior for others and reinforcing a culture of mutual respect.

At the heart of this paradox is the truth that boundaries, when paired with intentional focus, protect your energy and align your priorities. They create clarity in relationships, foster trust, and allow you to lead with confidence. By setting and honoring boundaries, you communicate respect for yourself and others, ensuring the right things receive your attention. Properly built, boundaries become invisible bridges strong enough to carry the heaviest loads.

One way they do this is by protecting your highest-value work. One of my favorite lessons is this: "**Don't be too busy to make money.**" Leaders often stay busy with activities that fill their day but don't move the needle. Effective boundaries ensure that your time and energy are spent on high-value opportunities, not just urgent demands.

This paradox reminds us that boundaries are about clarity and trust. Proactive boundary management, such as utilizing meetings and energy windows, is necessary to protect momentum. (In case you've never heard of an energy window, it's a simple but powerful concept: We have different levels of energy—what I call "energy windows"—throughout the day. You can protect your momentum by dedicating your strongest energy to your most important items. Similarly, setting up meetings outside of your strong energy windows helps you avoid the energy drain that so often comes with meetings.)

It doesn't stop there. This paradox speaks to the importance of addressing frustrations before they boil over. A conversation today prevents resentment tomorrow. Relationships where we let annoyances fester can reach breaking points in unexpected ways. By addressing issues early and setting clear boundaries, you strengthen your connections and foster deeper trust.

The lesson is this: Boundaries are the invisible bridges to success. They don't confine; they connect. They don't diminish relationships; they enhance them. Whether in love or leadership, boundaries guide us to where we are genuinely valued and help us create meaningful, enduring connections. They empower you to say yes to the right things—and to the people who matter most—by confidently saying no to what doesn't serve your purpose. And always remember, boundaries are meant to be helpful. The moment they stop serving you, they should be adjusted, not abandoned.

2.1. THE ART OF INTENTIONAL FOCUS

Leadership isn't just about what you take on—it's about what you leave behind. Setting boundaries and prioritizing intentional focus helps you identify what truly matters, shaping the boundaries that protect your energy.

I once realized that my most productive hours—6 a.m. to 11 a.m.—were being wasted on meetings. By shifting meetings to later in the day and dedicating mornings to deep, focused work, my productivity skyrocketed. This boundary didn't just protect my time; it elevated my leadership. My team also learned to consolidate their questions, coming to meetings better prepared and often solving issues on their own.

Sometimes, boundaries require more than just personal discipline—they necessitate intentional communication with those who help you achieve success. For instance, I had a right-hand person who was instrumental in navigating various challenges. Over time, I realized that sharing not just my objectives but also nuanced insights about individuals we worked with was crucial. I told her things like:

- "This guy is tempted to take advantage. Keep a firm grip on his accountability and help him build the right habits."

- "He'll say yes to everything, making you feel great, but he never meets deadlines. Don't rely on him for timely delivery, or he'll burn us."

This proactive boundary-setting was about protecting our collective focus and building trust in our team's ability to navigate challenges effectively.

Protecting yourself from distractions keeps your leadership sharp. Every time you allow low-impact tasks or undisciplined people to drain your focus, you weaken both your momentum and your mission.

I've seen firsthand how one person's lack of focus can paralyze an entire organization. I consulted for a company run by two brothers, and one of them constantly derailed progress. Whenever the team was close to a solution, he found an exception, raised a fear, or threw out an unrelated point that clouded the conversation and paralyzed the group. His hesitation regularly weakened momentum, eroded confidence, and hurt the business. I finally told him, "Your fears need to stop punishing the business." Leadership demands that we set boundaries and protect the team's clarity and momentum, not let personal doubts dismantle it.

When you focus on what matters most, every decision becomes a step forward. Focused leaders create momentum, align their actions with purpose, and inspire others to do the same.

Remember: Every yes to something unaligned is a no to something important. Boundaries built on focus ensure your energy is invested where it counts.

2.2. BOUNDARIES ARE BRIDGES, NOT BARRIERS

Connect by Saying No

Boundaries often get a bad reputation as walls that keep people out. In reality, they are bridges that strengthen relationships by clarifying expectations and fostering trust. Properly constructed, these boundaries not only hold the heaviest loads but also illuminate paths we might not have otherwise seen.

Consider a time when you didn't address a frustrating behavior because you liked the person demonstrating it. Maybe they interrupted you frequently or derailed your focus. Over time, those unspoken frustrations festered, damaging the relationship. Addressing these issues early—through respectful, boundary-setting conversations—can transform how you connect. When done thoughtfully, boundaries don't push people away; they bring clarity and mutual respect.

There's a story from my college days that underscores the transformative power of boundaries. I had a friend who was a magnetic, charismatic individual who could light up any room. One day, I found him visibly distressed. He'd been dumped by his girlfriend and was desperate to win her back. Seeing him like that, I asked him a question that would change his life: "Why do you want to date someone who doesn't want to date you?"

The question seemed simple, but it struck a chord. He paused, reflecting on what he truly wanted and deserved. Just days later, he met someone new. While I had to leave college for financial reasons and lost touch for a while, eventually he and I reconnected. By then, he was married to the very woman he met shortly after our conversation, and they had built a beautiful family together.

When we met again years later, he credited our brief exchange as a turning point. "Do you remember what you told me back in college?" he asked. I nodded. I truly couldn't have been happier for him. Their marriage hasn't been without its challenges, but the boundary each set of pursuing only those who genuinely wanted to be with them has guided them to lasting happiness.

This story embodies the essence of boundaries: They are not about exclusion but about creating space for what truly aligns with your values and purpose. Boundaries ensure that expectations are clear and respected. They create space for meaningful engagement, foster trust, and provide clarity in relationships—whether with clients, colleagues, or loved ones.

I see this play out in my own company all the time. Case in point: One of my employees has worked for me for years. She's a high performer, dependable, and someone I genuinely like. But recently, she's been slipping. Deadlines are getting missed, details are falling through the cracks, and the excuses are stacking up. A few years ago, I would have let it slide. I would have told myself she just needed time, and in the meantime, I'd pick up the slack. My rationale: I would have told myself I was protecting the relationship by staying quiet.

What I've learned, though—and what I hope you're learning too—is that silence isn't protection. It's slow poison. Avoiding boundaries doesn't save relationships; it erodes them. So instead of ignoring the issues, I asked her to sit down with me, and I told her the truth.

I said, "You're one of the best people I've got, but this isn't working. Here's what I expect. If you're overloaded, tell me. If you need help, ask early. But if you keep dropping the ball and I keep picking it up, we're going to have a different problem. I need you to be who I know you can be."

It was awkward. She didn't like hearing it, and I didn't like saying it. But a few weeks later, her performance turned around. She told me she felt relieved to know exactly where the line was. The air was cleared, the trust was stronger, and she stepped back into the standard she was capable of.

Boundaries at work don't shut people out. They make it safe to stay in the game together. They keep resentment from building in the shadows. They help good people stay good for each other.

When you lead, remember this: Connection is built through clear expectations and honest conversations. Sometimes the strongest bridge you can build is the one that begins with saying no.

2.3. MANAGING TIME

Lead with Clarity, Not Exhaustion

Leadership demands a tremendous amount of energy—mental, emotional, and physical. Without boundaries, you risk depleting yourself and becoming less effective for your team. Boundaries are the invisible bridges to success; when properly constructed, they can handle the heaviest loads. However, neglecting these boundaries can lead to burnout, conflict, or diminished results, as I've seen firsthand.

I once mentored a business owner who ran a high-end boutique. He was deeply committed to improving his team's performance and regularly immersed himself in the latest management philosophies. While his enthusiasm for growth was admirable, it often led him to adopt what I call a "management principle du jour" approach.

One particular instance stands out. He had read a book about aligning team performance with a revamped compensation plan. Inspired, he dove headfirst into the project, dedicating over two hundred hours to it. He read the book multiple times, held brainstorming sessions with his team, hired consultants, and meticulously drafted the new plan. In the end, though, it was a failure: His huge investment of time and money only impacted a handful of people, and they weren't even the focal point of the business! This is what happens when a leader gets high on theory and loses track of impact.

Imagine what could have been achieved if those two hundred hours had been redirected to coaching his team on improving their sales techniques or fostering deeper client relationships. His fixation on the project also created confusion and frustration within the team. The promised motivation and alignment never materialized. Instead, the team became overwhelmed by the constant shifting of priorities, and the boutique's performance suffered.

When we sat down to discuss the situation later, I asked him a simple but pointed question: "Would you pay your highest-paid employee to work on this project exclusively for five weeks out of the year?" He paused, then admitted that he wouldn't. That moment was a revelation. He realized that even good ideas need boundaries and that his time and energy had been misdirected. This story illustrates the pitfalls of boundary neglect. When leaders fail to set limits on their focus, they risk not only their own burnout but also a lack of clarity and direction for their team. Without boundaries, priorities blur, and the organization suffers under the weight of scattered efforts.

Contrast this with the benefits of proactive boundary maintenance. Effective boundaries allow leaders to focus on what truly moves the needle, ensuring their time and energy are spent on high-value activities. Leaders who set clear limits can confidently say no to ideas or trends that don't align with their overarching goals. This discipline protects against the fear of missing out (FOMO) and prevents the temptation to chase every shiny new concept.

To start getting focused in your own leadership journey, I encourage you to establish a time limit for exploring new ideas. Treat them as experiments with clear parameters. If they don't show promise within a defined period, move on. This practice ensures that ideas compete on merit rather than novelty, allowing you to protect your focus and maintain alignment with your strategic vision. At the same time, I suggest you conduct regular boundary reviews—both personal and organizational. This helps ensure that energy is invested wisely and time isn't wasted chasing fleeting interests.

Another effective way to protect energy is with the "standing meeting with an agenda." By consolidating nonurgent topics into scheduled discussions, you reduce distractions and empower your team to problem-solve independently. Over time, this approach fosters accountability, as team members learn to anticipate solutions rather than simply escalate issues. Meetings become moments of alignment, not interruptions, and leaders are freed from constantly putting out fires. The shift is profound—when people are given space to think critically and find their own answers, their confidence and decision-making skills grow exponentially.

The most successful and impactful leaders don't just manage their time—they manage their energy. Energy fuels momentum, creativity, and presence, making it far more valuable than mere efficiency. Remember those energy windows I talked about earlier? To operate at your best, you must understand your peak- and low-energy windows and structure your day accordingly. Identify when you're most productive and creative, then align your high-focus tasks with those periods. Organize your daily rhythm in a way that maximizes discretionary focus, ensuring that your most important work gets your best energy. Protect against energy leaks by empowering others where possible, reserving your energy for what truly moves the needle. Prioritize standing meetings in the right energy windows, allowing for deep work without sacrificing collaboration. And remember: Efficiency means little without effectiveness—true leadership requires not just productivity but also the intentional cultivation of relationships and trust.

2.4. MAINTAINING AND EVOLVING BOUNDARIES

I hope it's clear by now that your boundaries must remain strong, ensuring that leadership energy isn't wasted on low-impact tasks. Without clear limits, urgency overtakes importance, and reactionary work replaces intentional strategy. The best leaders set guardrails that protect their focus, allowing them to invest their time in what truly drives results. By making it clear when and how people can engage with you, you create a culture of respect, efficiency, and empowerment that benefits the entire organization.

At this point, you might be asking yourself what you should do with people's good ideas. We can destroy a lot of momentum and buy-in when someone has a great idea and it gets ignored. I've found it useful to create a "parking lot" for good ideas. We always have more ideas than we have the ability to execute, so capturing them and reviewing the list regularly ensures good ideas can be activated and others put on hold until the time is right.

At the same time, remember that boundaries require flexibility without compromising structure. Think of them as the steel beams of your leadership bridge—strong enough to support your aspirations yet flexible enough to adapt to shifting priorities. During peak periods, leaders may need to temporarily adjust availability for critical team needs, but always with a plan to recalibrate. Adapting to short-term pressures while maintaining long-term structure ensures that boundaries remain an asset, not a constraint. The key is knowing when to adjust and when to reinforce them to maintain stability and momentum.

One thing I've learned is that boundaries work best when they're helpful. They should make people feel safe, not scared. I've always had a clear time boundary at work: My team knows not to interrupt my deep focus blocks unless it's truly urgent. But they also know that if it really is urgent, they should come to me without hesitation.

One day, a team member called me while I was in the middle of one of my deep-focus sessions. She knew she did not need to be nervous, and she simply said, "Sorry to interrupt, but I have something urgent that needs your attention." She explained the situation—clearly and concisely—and I was able to give her the answer she needed in less than five minutes. It was an appropriate action on her part, and it demonstrated a fundamental truth: The main reason I set that boundary in the first place is to help us remain a great company, and her interruption helped us achieve that very thing.

Instead of shutting her down for "breaking the rule," I thanked her for having the courage to break it for the right reason. That conversation probably built more trust than weeks of perfectly "protected" time ever could. She knew the boundary was there for focus, but she also knew it could bend for the team's real needs.

That's the paradox: Boundaries need backbone, but they also need grace. If people feel like the only way to stay in your good graces is to be perfect, they'll hide mistakes or hold back when they shouldn't. That's where forgiveness comes in. It tells people they're more valuable than the offense. It shows them the boundary serves them—not the other way around.

Ultimately, boundaries enable leaders to focus on sustainable growth rather than the endless chase for new ideas or the exhaustion of constant availability. They ensure that every action is an investment in the vision you've set rather than a reaction to external pressures or fleeting excitement. By setting and maintaining clear boundaries, leaders create an environment in which they and their teams don't just survive—they thrive.

2.5. CONFRONT WHAT CORRODES TRUST

Sometimes the worst enemy of trust isn't conflict. It's unchecked assumptions. Far too often, those lead to situations where people take a poor interpretation of something and pin it on you as if you're guilty by association. Has that ever happened to you? If so, then you'll understand what I mean when I say this kind of situation feels like you're being punished for someone else's sins.

I used to pride myself on being tolerant, thinking it showed I was open-minded enough to let people say whatever they wanted, even if it was to rant about someone else. But I learned the hard way that venting can turn into poison when it crosses the line and attacks character.

I had a senior team member react strongly to a policy we needed to run the business better. She twisted it into the worst possible story—classic catastrophizing—painting me as someone who would do something destructive to her. Then, she threatened to quit. Instead of brushing it off, I sat her down and showed her how that storyline was not just wrong but corrosive. I made it clear that on my team, disagreement is fine. Public disparagement of my character (or anyone else's, for that matter) is not.

That conversation was uncomfortable, but it strengthened the bridge between us. Remember, boundaries don't push people away; they show exactly where trust lives and what will destroy it. Psychology calls this "rupture and repair" because you confront the rupture so trust can actually heal more strongly than before.

If you tolerate people's worst assumptions long enough, you will end up surrounded by wobbly supports that collapse the moment you need them most. Confront what corrodes trust before it rots the whole foundation.

TAKEAWAYS

Boundaries are not barriers; they are the bridges that connect us to what matters most. They protect our energy, clarify our relationships, and create the space needed for trust and respect to thrive. By learning to set and honor boundaries, leaders can lead with greater clarity, confidence, and authenticity. Use boundaries as the steel beams of your leadership bridge–strong enough to support your aspirations and flexible enough to withstand the weather of the moment.

Incorporating regular boundary reviews, utilizing energy windows, addressing frustrations early, and using tools like standing meetings and/or idea parking lots ensures that your boundaries evolve with your goals. When leaders embrace boundaries as acts of respect and connection, they foster trust, deepen relationships, and unlock the potential for lasting success.

Later in the book, you'll learn how to start building your own boundaries. And when you do, there won't be any more feeling trapped in commitments that drain you or in relationships that leave you depleted. After all, the ability to say no with confidence is what will allow you to say yes to the people and priorities that truly deserve your energy.

PARADOX 3

CLARITY IS COMPLICATED

WE ALL KNOW THE FEELING OF BEING PULLED IN TOO many directions. The mental tug-of-war between priorities, expectations, and uncertainty can be exhausting. When we feel torn, we second-guess our instincts, overanalyze what others might think, get lost in too many options, and hesitate out of fear of making the wrong choice. We get stuck. The way out of that? Clarity. And here's the thing: Context creates clarity. Not only that: Mastering your context accelerates clarity—and with it, decision-making.

Leadership demands clarity, especially when it comes to important decisions. Sometimes this means rejecting conventional wisdom. We cannot wait until all uncertainty disappears—because it never will. That's important to understand, deep in your being. Clarity isn't about eliminating doubt; it's about knowing how to move forward despite the doubt. It's about cutting through the fog and making decisions you can be proud of, even in complex, high-pressure situations.

One of my favorite sayings is, "**Your raise becomes effective when you do.**" It's a clever way to remind ourselves that clarity begins with self-awareness. You need to know where you currently stand and how to align with the direction your team, organization, or life is heading. Many employees miss this point, filling their days with busyness. Even more leaders and business owners do. Remember: Don't be too busy to make money.

Paradox 3 emphasizes the need for a leadership compass—a tool to guide you when complexity clouds the way. By the end of this paradox, you'll have taken the first steps to developing strategies to cut through the noise, align your actions with your vision, and build momentum.

There have been so many times I've felt pulled in too many directions. I often feel as if there are so many things I *could* be doing that it's hard to identify what to do first. If you experience this too, then you already know this can be overwhelming, even paralyzing. That's why we need to create our own reset buttons—reminders to stay grounded in our values and focused on our mission. This book is full of them—including one of my favorites, which is so apropos here: Accountability is crucial to keeping things clear.

Complexity is an inherent part of leadership. Between shifting priorities, diverse teams, and countless moving parts, leaders must master the art of navigating chaos without losing its nuance. True clarity means simplifying complexity without oversimplifying it.

This paradox will guide you to build your clarity by embracing complexity, distilling it into priorities, and creating tools to navigate with confidence. Get unstuck. Be you.

3.1. COMMUNICATING CLARITY

Leadership clarity is like a lighthouse in a storm—it doesn't calm the seas, but it does provide direction. At our company, we use a one-page strategic document to keep our focuses aligned with each other. This document includes long-term goals, two-year objectives, annual targets, and quarterly priorities. It also highlights obstacles and issues we foresee. Some items are measurable; others are principled. Each quarter, we revisit this document to ensure we stay on track.

Collaboration creates lots of ideas. And while many are good, done at the wrong time they can distract us. To address this, we created a "parking lot" (just like I described earlier) for ideas. Each quarter, we review these parked ideas to determine if they warrant action. This discipline has been a game changer for our team. By maintaining focus and resisting the urge to chase every new idea, we've consistently hit our annual goals.

Don't get me wrong: There are many factors in our success. However, this disciplined approach to clarity has been a cornerstone. These tools not only protect our efforts but also set clear expectations for the team, ensuring everyone knows what matters most at any given time.

Clarity in communication bridges the gap between intention and action. It's not just about being understood—it's about inspiring trust, focus, and momentum.

Imagine a master chef orchestrating a chaotic kitchen during peak service. To the diner, the experience feels seamless—a beautifully plated dish arrives with precision. But behind the scenes, the chef navigates a symphony of competing priorities: pairing flavors, coordinating timing, managing techniques, and addressing unplanned issues like dishes sent back to the kitchen or an impatient waiter. The chef's ability to distill this chaos into order is what creates an extraordinary dining experience.

I once spoke with the owner of a famous restaurant who shared a simple yet profound insight: His sous-chef focused on the bulk of the orders, while the head chef handled anything that came back for perfecting. This approach kept the head chef focused on the primary task and ensured customer satisfaction. Strong leadership mirrors this dynamic. Clear roles, well-communicated protocols, and intentional strategies help leaders manage the chaos while delivering extraordinary results. In leadership, the ability to filter noise and focus on the main objective is what turns daily chaos into lasting momentum. This level of clarity transforms complexity into something manageable, ensuring that each challenge strengthens rather than derails the team.

3.2. CONTEXT CREATES CLARITY

Failing to provide context is one of the most common leadership pitfalls. Early in my career, I learned this lesson the hard way. While managing a remodeling project, I left a crew without clear instructions. By the time I returned, they had done tasks out of order, creating inefficiencies that rippled across other projects. It wasn't their failure—it was mine. I hadn't communicated the overall objectives clearly or effectively, so they didn't have any context for what we were doing.

Providing context isn't about controlling every step— it's about empowering others to make decisions aligned with the bigger picture. Context builds collaboration and trust, allowing teams to offer ideas that align with organizational goals.

The example I just shared wasn't the last time I missed the "people/context" part of clarity. Years later, I learned an even more expensive lesson when a great idea died because my team didn't share my vision.

I developed a solution early on that should have catapulted our company forward. It would improve service and lower costs, and it was guaranteeable. On paper, it sounded too good to be true—except it actually worked. I spent months perfecting how to present it, built all the supporting documents, and even copyrighted the name. Everything looked bulletproof.

The problem wasn't the plan; it was the people. The team who needed to deliver it didn't believe in it. Some didn't understand it; others just didn't want to learn it. So it sat there for years—a perfect solution, dead on arrival. I thought clarity meant having the best idea and all the right words. But the truth is, clarity dies when people don't have the context or trust to carry it forward.

That failure taught me that your plan works only when the people executing it believe in it as much as you do. It was a hard lesson to learn, but it gave me the knowledge I needed to move forward differently. When I did, I was able to get buy-in, and our outcomes drastically improved. Clarity isn't just your logic—it's the connection you build so your team sees what you see and wants what you want.

Context is a powerful tool for alignment. By sharing the bigger picture and the reasoning behind decisions, leaders empower their teams to make better choices. This also fosters collaboration, as team members understand how their contributions fit into the larger vision. Without context, even the most skilled teams can falter. Communicating clarity requires empathy, foresight, and the ability to connect the dots for others.

Here are a few simple strategies for communicating context to teach your team.

1. **Provide Clear Logic**: When you explain the reasoning behind decisions, you do more than align actions—you teach critical thinking. By sharing the "why" behind decisions, especially when contrasting conventional wisdom with a more nuanced view, you can build important distinctions that strengthen team confidence. These conversations help team members understand the deeper dynamics at play, sharpening their judgment and preparing them to navigate complexity independently. It's not about justifying every decision; it's about seizing teaching moments that develop sharper, more decisive teammates.

2. **Tailor the Message**: Not every audience needs the same level of detail. To be effective, consider the recipient when crafting your message, focusing on what is appropriate and digestible for that group. A frontline technician may need to understand the immediate objective, while a senior manager may

need the broader strategic view. By tailoring the message to fit the audience—and speaking their language—you ensure clarity, avoid unnecessary confusion, and foster faster alignment.

3. **Encourage Feedback**: Saying a little less and inviting questions creates a more powerful communication dynamic than overloading people with information. When you encourage questions, you create space to better dial in your message, ensuring the recipient truly understands. Feedback loops catch misinterpretations early, strengthen relationships, and build a culture of continuous improvement. By welcoming clarification, you empower your teams to think critically, ask the right questions, and contribute more meaningfully to the mission.

4. **Clarify Authority**: Sometimes leaders need to explain themselves, but many times they do not. A common leadership mistake is forgetting the authority entrusted to you within the organization. When team members resist doing necessary work that aligns with their roles—stalling until they are fully convinced—you must recognize that the issue may no longer be about logic. It may be about reinforcing clarity around authority. To be effective,

you must know when to continue explaining and when to affirm expectations firmly, ensuring that clarity of mission outweighs endless debate.
   a. When you feel a conversation turning into endless debate, pause and remind yourself (and the team) of your authority. One simple way is to say, "I've heard everyone's input—now here's what we're going to do." Or, "I appreciate your perspective, but my decision is final because I'm responsible for the outcome."
   b. Sometimes all it takes is to remind your team that they are your team and are there to help you accomplish your goals. Otherwise, why would you have them on your team? Other times, it takes something firmer, like saying, "One way or another, I am going to get what I need." Your job as a leader is to discern the best approach and then deliver it in a way that is crystal clear and fits the context of the situation.

3.3. CLARITY SPEEDS UP DECISIONS

To me, being a good person and a good leader isn't about choosing between right and wrong—that's easy. It's about choosing between two goods. That's why prudence is my favorite virtue—it perfects the others.

I was once interviewed to join a business forum, a small group where peers build deep trust and lifelong relationships. During my interview, they asked about my business success. I answered honestly: "I way underperform my business potential."

Silence. I could see their confusion—they were all successful leaders who had likely grown up hearing, "A mind is a terrible thing to waste." The idea of choosing not to maximize potential was unthinkable to them. But I said it casually, as if it were obvious. They pressed me for more. I explained: Being home with my family is just as important as business success.

Most define success by what they achieve professionally. Not me. My life is more than what I do for a living.

In my twenties, I worked one-hundred-hour weeks. I was relentless—I never wanted to be broke again. When I got married, I kept that pace, coming home and immediately diving into work. My drive wasn't about ambition—it was about fear. Fear of failure. Fear of struggle. Fear of being broke again.

Then one night, my then-wife stopped me. She saw something I didn't. She knew this wasn't good for me, and she wanted to support me. She wasn't criticizing my work ethic—she was fighting for me.

Something clicked. I felt like I mattered.

That night, I made a decision: I would no longer let work consume my time at home. Full stop. I was ripping off the Band-Aid. When I was with my family, I was going to be with my family. No phone. No emails. No laptop on the couch.

I wasn't perfect—there were moments I broke my own rule. But I had my kids, so I knew I had to redefine my definition of success. Fatherhood is a top priority for me, and I couldn't have my definition of success exclude this important part of my life. I grew up without my parents, and I refused to be absent for my own children, no matter how much potential my business had.

As I shared all this with the group, I saw heads nodding. What had seemed like an admission of failure was actually my definition of success.

The truth is, I underperformed my business potential so that I could invest my time into the most important "potential" of all—being with the people I loved most (and still do). I went to work super early, stayed super focused while I was at the office, and protected my time so that when I was home, I was truly home. Sure, there were times when work crept into my family time, but I was mindful not to let the imbalance go too far for too long.

The moral here is simple: Get clear about what's important, then set your course and stick with it—until you can't.

There will always be unforeseen challenges and moments that demand adjustment, but a strong vision ensures you're making deliberate choices rather than reacting to every wave.

Remember, clarity is complicated, but by maintaining focus and adaptability, leaders navigate complexity with confidence and purpose. Decisive leadership requires balancing flexibility with commitment. It's about aligning decisions with values and goals while adapting to new information, without losing sight of what matters most.

3.4. CREATE A CLARITY COMPASS

I was once asked by the owner of a failing business for help in turning things around. That person had lots of experience, understood the industry, and really wanted to do a great job.

The first thing I did once I understood the situation: create what I call a "Clarity Compass" to guide every decision. The company was operating at an $800,000 loss, with unpaid vendors demanding payment. They had so many challenges they barely belonged in business. From how they operated, trained, and managed to how they handled basic functions like paying their bills, everything needed fixing. Even in paying bills, conventional wisdom said to pay the oldest first—but that approach didn't suit our situation. Instead, I prioritized vendors critical to our key client programs, protected the most profitable vendors, and negotiated discounts with others willing to settle. This strategy wasn't conventional, but it was clear: maximize cash flow, stabilize operations, and build trust.

I taught the accounts payable team to think strategically and approach their work like a profit center. The extra cash generated from negotiated discounts allowed us to pay off more vendors, and with that stability, I negotiated better rates going forward. This approach turned the $800,000 loss into an $800,000 profit within a year—without growing sales.

Clarity isn't about following standard advice—it's about knowing what truly matters and making bold decisions that align with your goals.

But clarity alone wasn't enough—the culture had to be rebuilt too. Fear, finger-pointing, and a lack of direction had corroded the team's ability to work together. Without addressing the underlying mindset, no amount of financial strategy would have been enough. We had to fix operations and rebuild belief at the same time. Much of the real work was mental: reestablishing trust, setting clear expectations, and building up a team that had been ill-equipped for the demands of a turnaround.

That turnaround remains one of the proudest accomplishments of my career—not because of the numbers, but because we changed what the team believed was possible.

The key: I used the power of clarity to help them set a direction, and I did it with just a handful of items that aligned people in a direction. By creating clarity and paying attention to sequencing, I was able to give them hope, create some short-term goals, do some longer-term rewiring, and provide them with ongoing support.

There are countless business clichés about how culture is more important than strategy. To me, the strategy was to build the right culture. Without anchoring the turnaround to a few clear principles and objectives, the fear and confusion would have overwhelmed any operational improvements we made. Strategy and culture are not competing priorities—they are inseparable.

That business's Clarity Compass helped them know what matters most and what to do first. It took into consideration how people were feeling, gave them things to focus on together, and instructed on how to keep everyone moving in the right direction. So remember, even as you're focusing on creating clarity, if the culture is not repaired and strengthened, it will eventually destroy whatever good work you are trying to accomplish.

3.5. SEE THE WHOLE PICTURE

I attended a retreat several years ago where we were given a ninety-minute block of silence for a nature walk. Each of us carried a worksheet filled with reflective questions designed to deepen our thinking. As I walked, I jotted down my answers, soaking in the surroundings while pondering the prompts. The path wound down to a serene pond, and at the end of the session, we gathered to share our thoughts.

One of the questions was tied to the walk itself, and I shared my perspective. I spoke about the experience of walking along the path, of winding my way down through the trees, of feeling the sun on my face. I talked about my experience contemplating the multitude of dramas that must have been playing out in the natural world around me too. The facilitator stopped the session and said he'd never heard anyone discuss the journey—most leaders talked only about the destination. He asked me why I reflected on the path, and I said, "There will always be more ponds. I like to remind myself of where I've been. It builds my strength." He pressed further, and I explained, "People look at the pond and see serenity. I see that too. But I also see it as a war zone—creatures attacking, hiding, hunting, and surviving. To me, it's fascinating to explore different perspectives."

That conversation reminded me that clarity isn't just about knowing the destination; it's about understanding the journey and appreciating the perspectives it offers. It also helped me realize something deeper about how I lead. If I see only the good in a situation, I miss the risks. If I see only the bad, I become a miserable person to be around. I need balance—because I live best with balance. My favorite virtue is prudence because it brings a level of balance to any situation. It helps me spot the good inside tough situations and identify risks even during great times. Being patient allows me to experience the good while properly addressing the risks without overreacting.

This mindset has shaped my leadership approach. As a CEO, my role is to nurture and protect the business—just like the role I see for myself as a father, a man, and a friend. Leadership clarity isn't about ignoring danger or exaggerating it; it's about seeing the whole picture and responding with wisdom. When you embrace the full complexity of a situation, you can lead with steadiness, resilience, and hope. That's real clarity. And it's complicated by nature.

3.6. TRUST THE PLAN

I touched on this briefly earlier, but it's worth exploring further here: Clarity in a business requires disciplined execution of leadership directives, even when team members feel tempted to adjust the plan, or don't fully understand it. Collaboration is valuable, but when a leader sets a clear direction, the team's role is to trust and execute—not renegotiate.

Clarity isn't complicated because people are bad; it's complicated because even good people can misinterpret when to collaborate and when to simply execute.

A good example of this comes from a firsthand experience I had with one of the managers at my company. I met with the whole management team and laid out a specific plan designed to improve client outcomes and reduce errors. Following it would reduce variables and help us better understand where breakdowns were happening. Everyone agreed and understood.

The next week, I had everyone come back in to review the process and its impact. One of the most experienced managers said, "I didn't have time to do what you wanted." I was stunned.

"What do you mean you didn't have time? I didn't create new work; I just wanted the work you were already doing done in a certain order," I said.

After a bit of back-and-forth, they finally admitted what was really going on: "I thought my plan was fine."

My response was direct: "You don't have permission to change instructions I give without my permission. Did you have permission?"

This wasn't about scolding—it was about aligning priorities, clarifying expectations, and creating accountability for the collective purpose.

Sometimes leadership work is collaborative, and sometimes it is instructional. Part of the complication is that people often don't recognize when it's one versus the other. When authority has made a clear decision, the role of the team isn't to debate or adjust it—it's to rally around it and execute it. Collaboration has a place, but clarity of mission requires discipline. When leaders allow constant renegotiation of direction, they surrender clarity, weaken momentum, and ultimately damage trust.

I look at it like this: The leader is the architect, carefully designing interconnected plans to make the business work. The manager, acting as a general contractor, doesn't have the full blueprint—only the portion needed to complete their work. If they start changing the structure based on partial knowledge, the whole project is jeopardized. Of course, not every decision needs full transparency to everyone; some elements are above certain pay grades or sensitive for broader business reasons.

Clarity sometimes demands following direction without persuasion, trusting that the architect is building something greater than what you can currently see. Leadership demands the team's courage to trust the plan—and the discipline to carry it out, even before they fully understand it.

3.7. COMPETENCE IS NOT ENOUGH

Sometimes clarity means drawing a hard line between what someone can do and who they really are when the pressure's on.

I once oversaw a manager who was outstanding at her work but terrible at owning responsibility when her team slipped. Anytime something went wrong, she'd separate herself from the outcome, point fingers, and stir up drama to keep the spotlight off her. She was half right, I suppose—after all, her people made mistakes—but her real pattern was classic psychological deflection. Instead of leading her team through mistakes, she pushed blame down and pulled pity up.

One day, she came into my office to ask for a promotion. I didn't sugarcoat my response. I told her, "In this company, advancement isn't just about results—it's about how you lead when things fall apart. We promote team builders."

Psychology calls this "reliable alliance." Trust is built when people know you'll stand with them when they mess up, not just stand above them when things go well. She had all the competence in the world, but she drained her team's safety instead of strengthening it. And no amount of training fixes that if you're unwilling to see it and change.

I gave her a clear path: Get the right training, adjust your approach, and become someone your people can count on to stand with them—not just above them. It was the push she needed to up her game.

Competence without trust is like a bridge with hidden cracks: It looks solid until the storm comes, then crumbles right when you need it most. So remember, competence gets you to the table. Character keeps you there.

TAKEAWAYS

The best leaders make complex items comprehensible. They create a Clarity Compass anchored in self-awareness and clear priorities to navigate through storms. I hope you will do the same. But remember, this compass cannot be effective unless you know where you are and where you'd like to go. Be self-aware. Be you.

You'll never have all the answers or completely erase doubt. And that's okay. Instead, focus on creating alignment, defining priorities, and empowering others to act with purpose. By mastering the art of clarity, you can cut through the noise, inspire confidence, and drive meaningful progress.

When you learn to do this, no longer will you be stuck in hesitation, paralyzed by the fear of making the wrong move. Because at the end of the day, clarity won't eliminate uncertainty, but it will give you the courage to act decisively, knowing that each step forward moves you closer to your vision.

PARADOX 4

FAILURE FUELS SUCCESS

WE'RE ALMOST HALFWAY THROUGH THE PARADOXES. How does it feel? I hope you're beginning to see how applying these truths to your life can make you a better, more centered, more aligned person—and a better, more centered, more aligned leader. That's certainly true for this next paradox, which deals with failure.

Failure is often seen as the enemy of success—something to fear, avoid, or even be ashamed of. We replay mistakes in our minds, worry about what others think, and sometimes even let failure reshape our sense of self-worth. But failure isn't the enemy. Failure teaches both endurance and its limits. It forges empathy and range in a great leader.

Let's face it: We've been conditioned to fear failure. We've seen people overblow missteps, weaponize mistakes, and use them as proof that someone is less than. This kind of thinking isn't just paralyzing—it's destructive. It teaches people to dodge failure like a poison arrow instead of recognizing it for what it truly is: a necessary step toward growth.

But the paradox of failure is that it's not a roadblock; it's a stepping stone. It's not necessarily a sign you're off track. Instead, it's often the path forward. The most successful leaders and organizations have learned to see failure not as an ending, but as raw material for progress. Major breakthroughs, innovation, and career-defining moments always have failure somewhere in their foundation.

To be clear, I am not encouraging failure for its own sake. I am saying failure should not be wasted. True growth emerges not from avoiding failure but from embracing it, learning from it, and using it as fuel for future success.

Imagine a seedling pushing through rocky soil; the obstacles it encounters strengthen its roots, allowing it to grow taller and withstand the storms it will inevitably face throughout its life. Leadership works the same way. Failures teach us, refine our strategies, and fortify our character. Learn to process your failures productively. Then do the same for others.

In the epicenter of failure, our greatest qualities receive the nourishment they need to grow. Resilience, humility, and creativity are all forged in the loneliness of failure. Far from being a signal to stop, failure is an invitation to dig deeper into our purpose, find strength in our vulnerabilities, and build strategies to rise again.

Like I'm sure you have, I've faced failures that initially seemed devastating but ultimately led to breakthroughs. Whether it was a lost client, a failed initiative, or a personal misstep, each failure carried a lesson that propelled me forward.

Here's the thing, though: Failure is useful only if analyzed and followed by action. It teaches leaders to develop a mindset of curiosity instead of fear, to face challenges with courage instead of hesitation, and to see setbacks as pivots, not end points.

This paradox isn't just about accepting failure—it's about transforming it. By the end of this paradox, you'll understand how to turn setbacks into momentum, mistakes into lessons, and struggles into stepping stones. Because real success isn't about avoiding failure—it's about learning how to rise from it.

4.1. RISE THROUGH FAILURE

We are conditioned to fear failure. But failure is not the opposite of success; it is a critical component of it. Leaders who fear failure often avoid risks, stagnating their growth and that of their teams. However, it doesn't have to be that way. Seen through a constructive lens, failure encourages curiosity over fear. To grow, we must view failure as a necessary ingredient for innovation and resilience.

This lesson got driven home to me early in my career. At the time, I was pursuing a large client that seemed like a perfect fit for our business. Despite months of effort and multiple pitches, we didn't win the contract. At first, I saw it as a catastrophic failure. But in the aftermath, I reviewed the process and discovered flaws in our approach—we hadn't fully understood the client's needs. This realization led to a complete overhaul of how we tailored our proposals. Within six months, we secured three new clients using the revised method. What felt like a failure was actually the turning point for growth.

This taught me one of my most enduring lessons: Failure is feedback. It's a mirror that reflects not just what went wrong but what can be made right. Had I wallowed in the loss, I would have missed the opportunity to improve. Instead, I turned failure into a strategy for progress.

That's the beauty of failure. It doesn't just reveal weak points in strategy—it reveals where your resilience will be tested.

Another early failure came when I worked on the largest project of my career. The company I was working for delayed payments for years, leaving me in a precarious financial position. This failure to collect on time drained all my profits from prior years and forced me to operate on credit while managing an overwhelming workload. Despite the pressure, I learned how to negotiate with banks, leverage real estate, and refine internal processes for accounts receivable and credit management. I also discovered how strong I was under pressure, and just as importantly, the power of asking for help when needed (not an easy lesson for someone who grew up like I did!). It was a pivotal moment that taught me that climbing the mountain of business success isn't about carrying the entire load yourself. It requires building relationships strong enough to lift you when you fall—and returning the favor when others need it.

Failure taught me endurance, but also the limits of endurance. You can stretch only so far before you need to adapt, strategize, and draw strength from others. In the end, failure didn't just make me tougher; it made me wiser. It taught me that the best leaders aren't the ones who never fall; they're the ones who learn how to rise stronger, surrounded by a team who believes in them.

4.2. THE GIFTS HIDDEN IN FAILURE

Failures help us understand ourselves better. In the Gospel of St. Luke, we learn how Peter, despite being warned he would deny Jesus three times, confidently declares he never will. Yet, as the story unfolds, Peter does exactly that, betraying the very conviction he held about himself. Imagine his shock—seeing himself as a leader, a protector, a believer, only to become a situational denier. But what a beautiful blessing this failure was for Peter. His denial became the bedrock upon which he built his faith, revealing his own humanity and the boundless grace of divine love.

Reflecting on Peter's story, I am reminded of how my own failures have been my greatest teachers. Just as Peter's denial wasn't the end but the beginning of his journey to become a pillar of the early church, each of my struggles has stripped away layers of pride, revealing a more authentic, empathetic leader within me. Through these trials, I've learned to love my neighbor more deeply, to see their struggles as mirrors of my own, and to lead with a compassion that only comes from having been humbled by falling down time and time again.

History is rich with stories of scientists, inventors, and business leaders who failed forward, eventually finding solutions that catapulted them to success. One of the great gifts of failure is that it teaches and reinforces humility. It's a balance: Success builds confidence; failure builds humility. When a leader has both, they become powerful.

I grew up very poor and attended just one year of college before I had to quit because I didn't have enough money even to eat. In the dorm, I was the only student without a phone. This wasn't unfamiliar—growing up, the absence of basic resources was normal. There was a phone company called Residence Communications, or Resicomm for short. When I started my facilities maintenance company, I named it Resicom so I'd never forget when I couldn't afford something as basic as a phone. For twenty years, I kept this story deep in my heart—like a gift to myself.

Remembering that struggle keeps me humble amid my business success. But it does more than keep me humble. It keeps me hungry. It reminds me that failure didn't finish me back then, so it won't finish me now. When I hit hard moments in business or feel the temptation to play it safe, I remember that kid who had to hustle just to have a phone line, and I remember I've come too far to shy away from hard things now. That experience is proof that I can survive setbacks, learn from them, and turn them into fuel.

You can learn to approach failure as a gift to yourself too. Because remember, humility born of failure doesn't make us smaller; it makes us indestructible.

Failures don't just build humility by softening pride—they build the kind of determination that makes leaders truly inspiring. Humility isn't about meekness; it's about recognizing the gifts we've been given and standing tall in them, even after falling. Being allowed to fail shows us we can survive the loss, survive the embarrassment, survive the disappointment—and that realization fuels an even greater courage.

I admire leaders who believe in themselves, who show up fully even after setbacks, who take action boldly without needing guaranteed applause. Their strength doesn't come from pretending they're invincible—it comes from knowing they are vulnerable and standing tall anyway. True leadership isn't about trying to gather as many followers as possible. It's about drawing the right people toward you—those who are inspired by your conviction, not your perfection.

When you've been humbled by your own failures, you stop fearing other people's failures too. You realize your job as a leader isn't to prevent every fall; it's to make it safe enough for people to get back up stronger.

One of the greatest gifts a leader can offer is safety—the kind of safety that gives others permission to fail, grow, and keep showing up. I was lucky enough to experience this firsthand myself. There was a man in my life who made me believe, without ever saying it outright, that if I ever got into a jam, he would be there for me. That unspoken promise strengthened me. It gave me the confidence to take risks, knowing that even if I fell, I wasn't alone. Great leaders do the same. Through their actions and humility, they let their people know, "You're safe with me."

I invite you to do the same. Remember, the people we are called to lead don't need a perfect leader—they need a courageous one. They need a leader willing to fall, rise, and walk with them through failure all the way to strength.

4.3. BUILDING RESILIENCE THROUGH SETBACKS

Resilience is the ability to bounce back from setbacks stronger than before. While failure is inevitable, it is resilience that determines how we rise. Leaders must model resilience for their teams, demonstrating how to recover, refocus, and move forward.

During the Great Recession, my retail facility maintenance business lost 80 percent of its revenue within two weeks. My top two clients shut down all work, leaving me scrambling.

When I lost that much revenue, I realized something simple but essential: I couldn't cut my way out of this—I had to sell my way out. Every dollar became precious. I had lived frugally even before the collapse, which helped, but I still had to prepare my family for the reality that we might have to sell our home. I wasn't going to cling to a lifestyle that would put us deeper into danger. Though I grew up without attachment to things—including where I lived or who I lived with—success had made me comfortable. Facing the possibility of losing that comfort was humbling. Thankfully, my then-wife had been raised with deep respect for living within her means, and her steadiness became a major source of strength. We pulled together, not apart, and battled through.

Failure also forced creativity in ways success never had. I coined a new strategy I called "unsolicited bids," driving through neighborhoods and industrial parks, quoting painting jobs for every home or building that needed it. I refused to sit back and wait for the market to come to me. Instead, I hunted opportunities. I showed my team through my actions that I was all in, no matter what. In doing so, I not only rebuilt the business—I reshaped the culture. We weren't entitled to success. We were willing to fight for it. Still, even fighters need something to believe in. For me, that belief came from an unspoken trust that I wasn't truly alone.

Remember the man I mentioned in section 4.2? Though he never came right out and said it, I truly believed that if I ever got into a bad spot, he would help me. That belief helped give me the confidence to do what I thought was right. I refinanced investment real estate to create a financial cushion and leaned on my belief that help was available if I truly needed it. While I never asked for that lifeline, believing it existed gave me the courage to keep pushing. And it paid off: Within two years, I had regained all the revenue I had lost and more. Maybe most importantly, I learned that adversity can lead to extraordinary growth.

Failure didn't just make me resilient; it made me resourceful, relentless, and real. It built the version of me that could weather any storm. I learned that storms don't destroy leaders—they reveal them. That's what resilience really is: finding a way, not an excuse. And true resilience isn't measured by how much you withstand; it's measured by how much you adapt, how much you lead, and how much heart you bring when everything's on the line. That's what failure taught me—and what failure gave me.

4.4. FAILURE FORCES INGENUITY AND STRENGTH OF CHARACTER

Failure doesn't just teach us to survive; it forces us to adapt, create, and ultimately thrive in ways success rarely does.

Early in my career, I didn't have the money needed to do everything the right way. I had to get creative. I negotiated better payment terms, partnered with companies, borrowed when I could, and learned how to do critical jobs myself to avoid extra costs. I stayed humble, asked questions, read everything I could, and leaned on the goodwill of others who saw my sincerity and determination. I didn't have enough money, but I had enough determination.

This scrappy, can-do spirit became one of the most valuable assets of my career. It built endurance, taught me how to outlast setbacks, and sharpened my ability to spot who had true perseverance and who didn't. Those lessons made me a better builder of teams and a better judge of character—skills that would shape every major success I later achieved.

Failure also reveals truths we might otherwise miss. I once helped a business where a destructive, arrogant team member caused constant frustration for the owner. The team member was talented but self-centered and resistant to feedback. While her mistakes were costly in the short term, they gave the team clarity about the culture they truly wanted.

When I stepped in, the owner was burned out and second-guessing herself every day. She'd known for a while that this toxic team member was holding the business hostage, but fear kept her stuck. I coached her through the real numbers, showed her what it was costing to keep one "star" while losing the trust of everyone else, and helped her script the conversation she needed to have with the difficult employee. She finally pulled the trigger and let that person go.

At first, it stung. A few clients complained, revenue dipped, and for a couple of weeks the owner wondered if she'd made a huge mistake. But within a month, the tide turned. Other toxic team members left, and the company began to thrive with less experienced—but far more coachable—team members who valued growth, humility, and collaboration. We got the team to share their ideas, implement what worked, and talk through what didn't. This helped us install better solutions and gave everyone a clearer understanding of why they were doing what they were doing. The team became aligned to the mission of the company.

That's an important lesson. As this example shows, oftentimes immediate setbacks feel painful. But they force necessary changes that wouldn't happen otherwise. They demand creativity under pressure and clarity about character. Failure doesn't just fuel success—it makes better success possible.

In the hands of a determined leader, failure becomes the forge that strengthens both the person and the team.

TAKEAWAYS

For too long, failure may have felt like proof that you weren't enough. But what if failure was never your enemy? What if it was always part of the blueprint that shaped you into the leader you are becoming?

Failure is not something to fear; it is something to embrace. Leaders who understand this paradox unlock the full potential of their teams and themselves. By reframing failure as a catalyst for growth, building resilience, and using setbacks to innovate, you can turn challenges into opportunities.

Remember: The difficult times of failure are the fires in which resilience is forged, character is clarified, and the foundation for lasting success is laid—not despite the struggle, but because of it.

PARADOX 5

ACCOUNTABILITY CREATES FREEDOM

THERE ARE SO MANY TIMES WHEN WE JUST WANT TO DO things the way we've always done them—without interference, without extra steps, without the burden of others slowing us down. Sometimes, that makes sense. There are plenty of things that should be done quickly, efficiently, and without added complexity.

But not everything works that way. We have responsibilities that go beyond just getting things done. We need to be accountable to who we are, our tasks, and our larger responsibilities.

In our key relationships, for example, we are often responsible for both protecting the other person and nurturing them to grow. The same is true in leadership—a manager or business owner is tasked not just with keeping things running, but with improving them, strengthening the team, and creating long-term success.

At first glance, accountability and freedom seem like opposites. Many people view accountability as restrictive, equating it with rules, oversight, and limits on their independence. They fear being locked into obligations, judged for mistakes, or held to expectations they may not always meet. So they dodge responsibility, shift blame, or remain vague about their commitments, believing this will give them more control over their own choices.

But dodging accountability doesn't eliminate expectations—it just removes clarity. And without clarity, people are left reacting instead of leading, defending instead of deciding, and scrambling instead of succeeding. Avoiding responsibility doesn't create freedom—it creates stress.

The same principle applies to personal accountability. Keeping ourselves accountable to being ourselves is another example. When we fail to act in alignment with our real character, we create unnecessary misunderstandings, frustration, and wasted energy. Instead of moving forward with confidence, we're left cleaning up confusion and hurt feelings, all because we weren't clear in the first place. Holding ourselves accountable to our own values isn't restrictive—it's what allows us to live with authenticity and peace.

Accountability doesn't benefit only individuals: It creates trust, alignment, and autonomy within entire teams. Others impose greater oversight on us when our behaviors are inconsistent. But when we are reliable and predictable in our commitments, we gain trust—and trust leads to freedom.

That's the paradox: The more accountable we are, the more freedom we earn. When people can count on us, they don't have to question us. When we consistently meet expectations, we are given more flexibility, not less. When we hold ourselves accountable, others don't have to.

I've learned that true leadership doesn't come from avoiding responsibility—it comes from embracing it. The more accountable I became, the more I was trusted. The more I followed through, the more autonomy I gained. The more I owned my actions, the more control I had over my success.

True freedom comes not from escaping expectations, but from earning trust through accountability. This paradox challenges us to rethink how we define freedom. Freedom isn't the absence of responsibility—it's the result of consistently meeting it.

5.1. A NEW DEFINITION OF SUCCESS

If you never considered the possibility that increased accountability can create more freedom, you're far from alone. Some people simply don't believe it, at least not at first. But what if you looked at accountability differently? Instead of seeing it as a limitation, you could see it as a framework that sharpens focus and unlocks true independence. As I often say, we need a more complex definition of success.

That may sound contradictory coming from someone who values clarity, but in reality, added structure actually increases focus.

A typical manager might define success as: *Get the job done on time and within budget.*

A better manager might say: *Get the job done on time, within budget, and at a level where the client would hire us again.*

But the best managers—the ones who understand accountability at its highest level—would say: *Get the job done on time, within budget, at a level where the client would hire us again, and in a way that strengthens and develops our team.*

See how the more complex definition of success actually improves execution? The additional "restrictions" make it sharper, more intentional, and ultimately more effective. Plus, the more consistently we deliver on these higher standards, the more our team members *and* our clients trust us—and the more flexibility and freedom we are given to lead independently.

When we consider things beyond efficiency—especially quality, relationships, and personal development—we create better solutions. Holding ourselves to a higher standard doesn't box us in; it gives us more control over our success.

People actively dodge responsibility because they believe that doing so keeps them free. But instead, it only creates confusion, stress, and wasted energy. Accountability is not a burden; it's a liberator. It sharpens focus, raises performance, and creates the very freedom people are chasing.

The paradox is simple: True independence comes from deeper responsibility, not less.

5.2. BEING ACCOUNTABLE TO OUR BLESSINGS AND AUTHORITY

To whom much is given, much is expected. This principle, rooted in scripture (Luke 12:48), speaks to the responsibility that comes with blessings—whether they be financial, intellectual, relational, or spiritual. Leadership is not just about making decisions; it is about stewarding what has been entrusted to us. Accountability to our blessings means using them wisely, not just for personal gain, but for the benefit of those around us. It also means recognizing that authority is not a privilege; it is a responsibility.

When leaders fail to be accountable for their blessings, they squander opportunities, misuse their influence, and erode trust. Before you ever see a business fail or a relationship break, you'll see smaller cracks: Trust erodes, teams grow resentful, opportunities slip through fingers, and energy drains away because people sense that blessings are being wasted or misused. Left unchecked, the consequences of this are profound: failed businesses, broken relationships, and mismanaged resources. But when leaders embrace accountability for their blessings, they unlock the full potential of their blessings. They create environments in which people thrive, resources are used wisely, and success is multiplied.

Leadership is a paradox. On one hand, it provides influence, authority, and the ability to shape outcomes. On the other hand, it comes with immense responsibility. Many seek to become leaders for the benefits, but few fully grasp the accountability that accompanies it. Every decision a leader makes carries weight, not just for themselves but for those they lead. A single choice can inspire or discourage, build or destroy, uplift or oppress.

I have seen many leaders struggle under this weight. Some avoid making tough decisions, hoping problems will resolve themselves. Others become overly rigid, clinging to authority without reflection. The best leaders, however, recognize that their role is not about power—it is about stewardship. They understand that leadership is a calling, not a status, and that accountability to their blessings is what defines their legacy.

One of the most powerful lessons I learned about being accountable to my blessings came through an unexpected source: an annual Christmas event we put on for families living in poverty. Initially, our focus was on providing gifts, meals, and warm clothing for the children. But as the years went on, I realized we were missing something. The parents were often overlooked, standing quietly in the background as we celebrated their children.

This realization changed everything. We began offering parents new coats, purses, and other items—not just as handouts, but as dignified gifts to remind them that they too mattered. Over time, the event evolved beyond simply meeting material needs. We recognized that our responsibility was not just to provide, but to uplift: to restore dignity, to create moments of joy, and to remind people of their worth.

This reinforced to me that blessings are not meant to be hoarded; they are meant to be shared. A leader who clings to wealth, knowledge, or influence without using it for the benefit of others is not truly leading. When we are accountable to our blessings, we recognize that they are tools, not trophies. They are given to us so that we can create opportunities, not just for ourselves, but for those who come after us.

Our biggest blessing is ourselves...our time, talent, and treasure. Every day, we get the chance to bring those gifts into our communities: family, friendships, workplaces, faith communities, and neighborhoods. Showing up with generosity and integrity makes us a blessing that multiplies. A word of encouragement, an extra hour invested, a skill freely shared—these are small acts that ripple out in ways we can't always see. Wherever you are, plant good seeds and trust they'll grow.

Faith plays a crucial role in this accountability. Throughout my life, there have been moments when I questioned why certain doors closed or why I faced specific challenges. But in hindsight, I see that those moments were shaping me, teaching me how to use my blessings with greater wisdom. Leadership requires a long-term perspective—one that acknowledges that what we have today is preparation for what we will need tomorrow.

At its core, being accountable to our blessings is about freedom. When we embrace responsibility, we are no longer burdened by fear, doubt, or hesitation. We make decisions with clarity, act with conviction, and lead with purpose.

The world does not need more leaders who seek power. It needs leaders who embrace responsibility—who understand that true influence comes not from what we gain, but from what we give. By being accountable to our blessings and authority, we do more than lead. We inspire.

5.3. FOSTERING TEAM-WIDE ACCOUNTABILITY

Leaders aren't responsible only for their blessings. They are also responsible for their authority. Leaders who fail to be accountable to their authority often fall into two traps: abuse or negligence. Some wield authority recklessly, making decisions based on ego rather than wisdom. Others avoid responsibility altogether, failing to lead when leadership is most needed. Neither approach serves the greater good.

True authority is not about control—it is about empowerment. It is about creating environments in which people can grow, teams can flourish, and success is measured not by individual achievement, but by collective impact. Leaders who understand this recognize that their authority is not about them—it is about the people they serve.

Further, accountability is not a solitary act; it is a culture. Leaders who are accountable to their blessings create teams that are likewise accountable. They set the standard through their actions, demonstrating what it means to steward resources, make wise decisions, and lead with integrity.

A company or team that lacks accountability will drift into dysfunction. Deadlines will be missed, clients will lose trust, and mediocrity will become the norm. On the other hand, a culture of fear-based accountability—where mistakes are met with immediate consequences but no guidance—will crush morale and stifle creativity. The healthiest teams are those that see accountability as a tool for empowerment, not punishment.

When people know where they stand, when expectations are clear, and when justice is applied with wisdom, they are free to perform at their best. They are not constantly second-guessing themselves, nor are they weighed down by fear of arbitrary consequences.

Accountability gives people confidence that their work matters and that their contributions are recognized. It ensures that success is earned, not given. And most importantly, it provides the framework for trust. When people know that they will be held responsible for their actions—but also supported in their growth—they develop the confidence to take ownership of their work.

Leaders must model prudent accountability themselves. If a leader expects diligence but is frequently late or disorganized, their credibility is weakened. If they demand high standards but never acknowledge effort, resentment will build. On the flip side, though, leaders who practice what they preach set a standard that inspires others to follow.

One of the most effective ways to build a culture like this is through transparency. When leaders openly discuss their responsibilities, challenges, and the reasoning behind their decisions, they invite others into the process. This creates trust, fosters collaboration, and ensures that accountability is not seen as a burden, but as a shared commitment to excellence.

Of course, transparency also needs boundaries. Not every detail serves your team. A simple rule is this: Share what clarifies expectations, builds trust, or helps people do their jobs better, and keep private what distracts, overwhelms, or sows unnecessary doubt.

True accountability starts with leaders who own their authority wisely and share it generously. When you pair that with clear, purposeful, and wise transparency—the kind that's rooted in your own integrity and your commitment to protect what your people need to thrive—you create a culture where trust runs deep and people rise to do their best work.

5.4. STRUCTURE THAT ENCOURAGES ACCOUNTABILITY

Ambiguity is the enemy of accountability. When people do not know what is expected of them, they either hesitate to take initiative or operate in silos. Both outcomes stifle progress. The best way to prevent this is to ensure that every team member understands their role, their responsibilities, and how their work contributes to the bigger picture.

Accountability does not happen by accident—it requires structure. Without a clear framework, accountability can feel inconsistent, unfair, or even oppressive.

But when structure is built with intention, it creates an environment in which accountability is not just accepted but embraced. The right structure removes ambiguity, provides clarity, and empowers people to take ownership of their actions.

Many leaders struggle with accountability because they lack the right systems. They expect results without defining expectations, they demand responsibility without providing guidance, and they enforce standards without offering support. The result is frustration, misalignment, and wasted potential. However, when accountability is built into the structure of an organization, it is no longer an external force imposed upon people. It becomes part of the culture.

Structure is not about control; it is about liberation. A well-structured team knows who is responsible for what, understands how success is measured, and has the support needed to meet expectations. This creates confidence, reduces unnecessary stress, and allows people to focus on what they do best.

One of the best lessons I learned about structure came when I was reorganizing my company. As we grew quickly, people wore too many hats, roles overlapped, and decisions fell through the cracks. What once worked when we were small no longer fit who we had become.

At the time, roles were unclear, accountability was inconsistent, and inefficiencies were everywhere. People were working hard, but without direction. The problem wasn't effort—it was structure. I remember looking around and realizing we were spinning our wheels: Projects were late, team members were frustrated, and small problems snowballed into big ones because no one really knew who "owned" what.

It wasn't easy to fix. People worried about losing authority or having to learn new ways of working. I faced a lot of resistance, but I didn't let that deter me. Instead, I tackled it piece by piece, mapping out every role, clarifying who was responsible for what, and setting up regular check-ins to catch problems early. It took months to get it right, but every adjustment brought more trust and more calm.

By redefining roles, clarifying responsibilities, and implementing regular check-ins, everything changed. Performance improved, stress levels dropped, and accountability became a natural part of our operations.

At first glance, structure might seem like a limitation. But the irony and the paradox is that the right structure creates freedom. It removes uncertainty, fosters trust, and allows people to operate with confidence. And when that happens, accountability is no longer feared—it is embraced as a tool for success.

By creating a framework where accountability is clear, fair, and consistent, you can unlock the full potential of your teams. You can cultivate an environment in which people are not just working, but thriving—in which accountability is not a burden, but a pathway to excellence. In short, you can build a structure that turns chaos into confidence.

5.5. PRUDENT DECISIONS— THE ESSENCE OF ACCOUNTABILITY

In leadership, accountability means holding others to a standard in a way that balances justice and mercy. Too much rigidity, and we push people away. Too much leniency, and we create disorder. St. Thomas Aquinas reminds us that: "Mercy without justice is the mother of dissolution; justice without mercy is cruelty." The key is in knowing when to challenge, when to support, and when to adjust.

Prudence is the perfecter of virtues. It is the guiding force that determines when to act with justice and when to extend mercy. It ensures that accountability is not wielded as a weapon but applied with wisdom to cultivate growth. Accountability without prudence can be destructive—it can erode trust, discourage initiative, and instill fear rather than confidence. Leaders must navigate this balance carefully, holding people responsible in ways that encourage improvement rather than paralyze them with anxiety.

Leaders who fail to practice prudence often find themselves oscillating between extremes. Some become too rigid, enforcing accountability with an iron fist, leaving no room for human error, growth, or redemption. Others go to the opposite extremes, failing to enforce standards, tolerating mediocrity, and avoiding difficult conversations for fear of conflict.

Both approaches lead to dysfunction. The prudent leader, however, discerns when correction is necessary and when grace is the better path forward. By understanding this balance, leaders transform accountability from a burden into a tool for empowerment.

Consider an employee who consistently underperforms but has great potential. A leader focused purely on justice might immediately terminate them, arguing that accountability demands it. A leader focused solely on mercy might tolerate the poor performance indefinitely, hoping things improve. The prudent leader, however, recognizes that the right course of action depends on context. Has the employee been properly trained? Are they aware of the impact of their mistakes? Is this a pattern or a temporary struggle? Accountability means holding them responsible, but with a strategy—offering support where needed while making it clear that expectations must be met.

The Gospel of John provides a powerful illustration of this balance. In John 8:1-11, the Pharisees bring a woman caught in adultery before Jesus, demanding justice in the form of her execution. Instead of immediately responding, Jesus pauses, writes in the sand, and then speaks a truth that forces self-examination: "Let him who is without sin among you be the first to throw a stone at her." His words uphold the law while also revealing the hypocrisy of her accusers. One by one, they leave. Once alone with the woman, Jesus does not dismiss her sin, nor does he condemn her. Instead, he offers mercy with accountability: "Go and sin no more." This moment exemplifies prudence—justice and mercy in perfect balance.

Leaders face similar moments when the right response is not always the obvious one. When confronted with failure, misconduct, or underperformance, a leader's goal should not be simply punishment, but restoration. Accountability is not about punishing the past; it is about improving the future. Holding people to a standard must come with the tools and support to meet that standard. When leaders practice this, they create an environment in which accountability fosters confidence, not fear.

5.6. IMPACT TO FUTURE BEHAVIOR

As I've mentioned, accountability should build strength, not fear, and real strength is always rooted in wisdom. Like section 5.5 shows, prudent leaders do not rush to judgment. They gather information, make sure they understand the context of the situation, and evaluate possible outcomes before making a decision. This ability to pause and assess makes all the difference between reaction and response. A well-timed word of correction can change a person's trajectory, just as an ill-timed rebuke can crush their spirit.

Accountability must always be tied to clear expectations. If someone fails, the first question should be, "Was the expectation clear?" If not, accountability needs to begin with better communication. If expectations were clear but not met, then accountability requires assessing why. Was it due to negligence, lack of skill, or external factors? Understanding the cause determines whether the response should be correction, additional training, or realignment of roles.

Prudence also means recognizing that fairness and equality are not the same. Treating everyone the same regardless of circumstances is not prudent—it is lazy leadership. People have different strengths, weaknesses, and situations that require different approaches. That's why the goal of accountability should not be uniform punishment or reward but individualized growth.

When I was in my forties, I encountered a difficult test of this principle. A trusted associate managing investments stole an impactful amount of money from me. I was faced with two choices: pursue legal action and hold him to justice in its purest form, or take another approach. I did what I thought was prudent. I confronted him, expressed my disappointment, and told him I no longer trusted him. Instead of immediately seeking retribution, I gave him three months to find new employment. I also forgave him. This wasn't about excusing his actions; it was about holding him accountable in a way that preserved both my integrity and his opportunity to move forward.

I never got the money back. And he didn't change—in fact, he stole even more during those three months. When I discovered that, I knew I couldn't help him anymore. I turned the matter over to the authorities, not because I sought revenge, but because I needed to draw a clear line and protect my business. Some people will grow when you hold out your hand; others won't. My peace comes from owning my behavior—not someone else's outcomes.

That decision reinforced a key lesson: Accountability should be measured not just by consequences but by the impact it has on people's future behavior, including your own. If I had reacted purely with justice, I might have satisfied my anger, but I would have severed the opportunity for growth. On the other hand, if I had done nothing, I would have failed in my duty as a leader to protect the integrity of my business. Sometimes prudence means giving grace, and sometimes it means drawing a hard boundary. Often it's both.

I don't know what tests you'll face, but I do know this: Your integrity is worth more than the dollars you might lose. Being accountable means you handle the truth, protect what matters, and keep yourself intact.

5.7. PERSUASIVE WILLPOWER AND ITS UNEXPECTED SHADOW

Willpower is powerful. Just ask all the people I've overwhelmed through the years! One of the shadows of my younger self's "no-matter-what" approach was that it could bulldoze people down without me even noticing. I first caught a glimpse of it with a friend of mine. In the middle of an argument, he just shut down. He had a point to make but decided I wasn't worth the trouble. He liked me, but he didn't want to be on the receiving end of my force. Without a word, he gave me an insight I couldn't shake, but I didn't yet know what to do with it.

A few months later, it all clicked. I was sitting across from a man I'll call James, the CEO of a much larger company we were thinking about partnering with. He used his persuasive willpower like a battering ram, talking endlessly, reciting credentials, pounding away any room for pushback. In each area that I asked a question, he worked to show me he already knew the answer. It wasn't exactly my style. I had always used willpower to expose other people's weaknesses, not to inflate myself. But the flavor was the same: raw force draining the trust right out of the room. Instead of seeing his intensity as passion, I saw fear. I knew he would be easy to work with, as long as you agreed with everything he said. And in that moment, I saw myself in him.

Sitting in James's office that day, I learned that persuasive willpower works until it doesn't. When it is misapplied, it signals distrust, ignores other people's perspectives, and leaves wreckage behind. I finally realized accountability isn't just about owning the outcomes—it is about owning how you use your strengths. If you are going to run at 100 mph, you had better take care of the engine and the mechanics who keep it running. True freedom comes when you can harness your willpower to build, not bulldoze.

Create your freedom through accountability. Understand your powers and use them wisely. Perhaps most of all, find your strengths and learn what works until it doesn't.

TAKEAWAYS

Accountability is not a burden; it is a pathway to true freedom. When we embrace it, we gain clarity, trust, and alignment with our values, allowing us to lead and live with confidence. Making prudent decisions, being accountable to our blessings, and creating structures that reinforce responsibility liberate us from chaos and uncertainty. Instead of feeling constrained, we become empowered to operate with purpose, knowing our actions are rooted in wisdom and integrity.

True freedom is not found in avoiding responsibility but in owning it—understanding that discipline and trust create the foundation for growth and fulfillment. By mastering this paradox, we transform our perspective on leadership and life. We recognize that accountability is not something to resist but something that elevates us, enabling us to operate at our highest potential. It fosters trust, strengthens relationships, and ensures that we remain aligned with what truly matters. If avoiding accountability has left you overwhelmed, uncertain, or stuck in cycles of frustration, it's time to take ownership. True confidence comes not from escaping responsibility but from embracing it, knowing that accountability clears the path for freedom, stability, and real success.

When we hold ourselves and others accountable with justice, mercy, and prudence, we create a world where freedom is not the absence of structure but the result of it—where individuals and teams flourish and where we step fully into the people and leaders we are meant to be.

PARADOX 6

POWER GROWS WHEN IT'S GIVEN AWAY

POWER IN LEADERSHIP IS OFTEN ASSOCIATED WITH control and decision-making authority. But—and here is paradox 6—true power doesn't come from holding on tightly; it grows when you give it away. By empowering others, you multiply their impact, build stronger teams, and create sustainable success. When you share your power, you enable your teams to lead, innovate, and thrive. And here's the hidden benefit: You also free yourself. By letting go of unnecessary control, you reclaim time, mental energy, and the ability to focus on higher-impact work. You stop putting out fires and start setting the vision. The freedom you gain helps everyone do better.

Why, then, do so many people struggle with this? The answer is simple: Many leaders convince themselves they are the best at what they do, that things must be done their way, and that delegating is too risky. They believe that by controlling everything, they will ensure success. So they micromanage, struggle to trust others, and take on too much. Even when they are drowning in responsibilities, they refuse to ask for help. Even worse, many think the solution is to find a "clone" of themselves—someone who can do exactly what they do, in exactly the same way. But this is not optimization. The truth is, optimization happens when tasks are done better, faster, or smarter—and not necessarily by you. When leaders hold on too tightly, they become the bottleneck to their own success.

Before we go any further, let's face the fact that **delegation is only powerful when done well**. Giving away power isn't abdicating responsibility; it's about developing others, building trust, and creating a culture where people feel empowered to take ownership of their work. Delegation is a profound sign of respect. Trust is built when one person entrusts another with something important. A strong, cohesive team is a leader's greatest asset—and it's built by giving power away. It requires more than handing off tasks; it demands seeing the good in others, investing time and care, and trusting them to grow. After all, we wouldn't entrust anything important to someone we didn't value. Empowerment can feel messy at first, but leaders willing to share their power build teams that are loyal, capable, and ready to multiply success.

This isn't just a theoretical principle. In my journey, I've experienced it firsthand, over and over. I've learned that holding on to power too tightly stifles creativity, limits growth, and leads to burnout. By learning to share power effectively, I've seen teams flourish, leaders emerge, and results exceed expectations.

This paradox challenges us to rethink how we use our influence and embrace the strength that comes from empowering others. Strong leadership isn't measured by control—it's measured by how much you lift others up. Your leadership multiplies when you give others the power to rise.

6.1. EMPOWER THROUGH DELEGATION

The "how" of anything—especially delegation—matters. Great leadership develops people while still making sure that tasks get done, and done well. Helping people be themselves is one of the most beautiful gifts you can give someone. Each of us brings something special to the table. True leadership embraces everyone's authenticity, especially our own.

As I said at the beginning of the book, the best advice I ever gave myself is "Be you!" It's a lesson beautifully echoed in Matthew 5:13, where we're reminded of our value and authenticity through the metaphor of salt: "You are the salt of the earth, but if salt loses its saltiness, how can it be made salty again? It is no longer good for anything, except to be thrown out and trampled underfoot." What I love most about this passage is how it calls us to embrace who we are meant to be. Even more, I love the overlooked part—it acknowledges that the parts of us that don't align with our true essence still serve a purpose: They teach us the practice of throwing things out and trampling them underfoot.

This scripture challenges us to let go of the parts of ourselves that don't align with our purpose, to refine our talents, and to discard habits that don't serve us. It connects deeply to my leadership journey, where I've realized that, like salt, my purpose is to enhance the world around me and leave people better than I found them. There have been so many times in both my personal and professional life when I achieved success but felt unfulfilled, especially when I went along to get along. The problem: I wasn't being myself, and because of that, no matter how outwardly successful I appeared, it didn't feel meaningful.

There's no question that letting go of control is one of the hardest but most rewarding shifts a leader can make. When leaders micromanage, they may feel productive, but they're often limiting their team's potential. Empowering others requires trust, clarity, and intentionality.

Early in my career, I struggled to let go of control. I felt that if I wanted something done right, I had to do it myself. My two key guys and I used to talk about how we wanted to clone ourselves. But you know what? We were wrong. We only needed to be the ones to do it because we didn't empower others. Sure, we trained them, but we never really trusted them. Our reluctance to delegate wasn't protecting my business—it was holding us back.

Once I realized that, I knew I needed to make some changes. I started small, entrusting key decisions to individuals on my team. What I found was astonishing: Their solutions often surpassed my expectations. They brought perspectives I hadn't considered and took ownership in ways I hadn't anticipated. For instance, I developed a powerful way to present our solutions, a method so compelling that it seemed to sell itself. At first, I thought I should always be the one who presented it to clients because I knew the program inside and out. However, I realized that the right person could achieve even greater results. I trained a team member who had the perfect combination of intelligence, personality, and disposition. She presented with authenticity and connected better with clients than I ever could. My role shifted to supporting her as a subject matter expert. This not only elevated her value to the team but also strengthened our relationship and drove superior results.

The lesson here: Great leaders don't just manage tasks; they develop people. Transitioning from a great worker to a great leader means shifting your focus from individual performance to team success. This requires intentionality and a willingness to invest in others.

Empowering others makes you stronger.

6.2. DELEGATE TO ELEVATE

Empowering people includes delegating responsibilities and giving people ownership of tasks and outcomes. I once worked with a team member who was hesitant to take on more responsibility. They were capable but unsure of their ability to lead. Instead of pushing them, I shared my confidence in their potential and gave them a small, high-visibility project. I also made it clear that mistakes were acceptable as long as lessons were learned.

The results were everything I hoped for—and expected. Their initial hesitation melted into determination. They delivered the project with excellence and, in doing so, transformed their view of their own capabilities. This experience reinforced a key truth: Trust is the currency that enables people to step into their own power. By giving trust generously, leaders cultivate a culture where growth and innovation flourish.

One great way to empower others is through entry-level positions. At Resicom, we manage a portfolio of rental properties and had been employing college students for tasks like yard work, painting, and minor repairs. But it soon became clear that we could delegate so much more to them.

At the time, our property managers were overwhelmed, juggling tenant issues, property acquisitions, and all the associated administrative work. During a heated meeting, as the head of real estate was about to leave for yet another tenant meeting, I suggested she delegate this to one of our young technicians. The suggestion came from a moment of frustration, but it was a sound idea. She was hesitant but complied. The outcome was astonishing—the tenant was satisfied, and it sparked a revelation for our team: If you don't trust and teach your team, you'll spend most of your time putting out fires, and that's the last thing you want your leaders doing.

This experience prompted us to reassess the capabilities of our entry-level staff. Within two weeks, we developed a training program that empowered half our technicians to handle tasks previously reserved for property managers. This not only multiplied the efficiency of our property managers, allowing them to focus on strategic roles, but also significantly reduced response times to tenants. By elevating these young workers, we transformed what were once seen as basic roles into pivotal positions that directly enhanced our operational effectiveness.

Empowerment is about unlocking the greatness hidden in your team. Freeing up your time is the cherry on top. When you give people a real chance to rise, they often soar further than you ever imagined.

6.3. DEVELOP LEADERS THROUGH THE WORK

As we've seen, sustainable leadership is about giving away power, not holding on to it. Delegation is a tool that elevates everyone's performance. It's more than handing off tasks; it's about creating opportunities for the whole business to grow. One of the most effective ways to build leadership capacity is through initiatives. By assigning team members responsibility for key projects, you give them the chance to step into leadership roles. This not only develops their skills but also demonstrates your trust in their capabilities.

I once assigned a team member at Resicom responsibility for vendor negotiations, but with a twist: She could lead the process, but she had to empower others to be the negotiators. Sure, if I'd had her handle the negotiations herself, they would have been done properly, quickly, and effectively. But when you're building a team, you need to intentionally develop your people. I like to say, "We develop our people through the work." That means we take advantage of live situations to strengthen our team.

The directive I gave her—to elevate others to negotiate instead of handling everything herself—was counterintuitive; she was a strong negotiator. But I stuck to my guns. The project was messy at times as people didn't follow her direction perfectly, mistakes were made, and simple points were missed. If we looked at the task purely as "get negotiations done," we never would have done it this way. But when we viewed it through the lens of leadership development, we absolutely did it right.

This initiative forced her to move from doing the work to building others who could do it. Before we kicked it off, I explained exactly why we were doing it this way: that the goal wasn't just to get deals done, but to grow more people who could do them well. She had to consider the people involved—their skills, gaps, and potential—and find ways to help them succeed. She created tools they could reference without needing constant hand-holding. She had to encourage them, celebrate their wins, and stay patient when mistakes happened. In the end, she didn't just complete a project; she strengthened her relationships with the team, saved the company money, created a training guide for future negotiators, and built a repeatable model for scaling excellence. She also elevated her own leadership skill set. It was a win for her, for the people she trained, and for the company.

Empowerment isn't just a buzzword—it's a life-changing approach to leading. I've had team members tell me that being trusted with a major initiative was the turning point in their career. It wasn't the project itself that changed them; it was the belief I placed in them. That belief sparked a confidence that shaped the leader they became.

Ultimately, the greatest leaders aren't remembered for what they accomplish alone but for how they elevate others. Legacy isn't built through control; it's built through empowerment. By relinquishing control, you don't just lighten your workload; you unlock your team members' potentials.

Bottom line of this paradox: Delegating important initiatives develops many. When you focus on elevating your team instead of showcasing your own ability, you unlock a deeper power: a stronger, more cohesive team. That's when leadership truly multiplies.

6.4. DEVELOP RANGE AND BUILD FLEXIBILITY

As leaders, building up organizational capacity is critical, but the path to achieving this isn't always about hiring more staff or relying heavily on highly paid specialists. Instead, a more effective approach lies in developing range within your existing team. For example, rather than bringing in an exorbitantly compensated CFO, a well-trained accounting team—supported by an external accounting firm and following clear monthly protocols—can handle financial management effectively.

Similarly, human resources doesn't always need a specialized department. A structured human resources process, coupled with managers who genuinely care about their people and backed by a law firm specializing in unique human resources situations, can significantly streamline operations while reducing dependency on highly compensated staff.

This strategy achieves two things. First, it manages costs by avoiding the overstaffing of niche positions. Second, it fosters a dynamic, versatile workforce where individuals grow into owning broader responsibilities, creating flexibility in roles and enabling the team to ebb and flow with the business's needs. By focusing on leveling up the skills of your existing team, you're not just building capacity—you're empowering your people to step up and meet challenges, which fosters engagement and loyalty.

Creating flexibility in roles is a cornerstone of building a resilient organization. When individuals aren't confined to their "sandbox," they have the opportunity to grow in areas that align with both the company's evolving needs and their personal strengths. This adaptability makes the team more integrated, dynamic, and capable of handling a variety of challenges. For example, in our company, retention is not the sole responsibility of one department (say, human resources). Rather, it falls squarely on the shoulders of all our managers across departments. Managers must take ownership of their team's growth and satisfaction, ensuring alignment with our values of empowerment and development. As part of that, we focus on promoting individuals who are not only strong performers but also exceptional trainers and mentors. These leaders have a knack for launching careers and encouraging potential, steering clear of the command-and-control style of management.

This emphasis on relational leadership strengthens our team's foundation and ensures long-term loyalty. It's not just about keeping people employed—it's about fostering a sense of purpose and alignment with the organization's mission. By empowering managers to take the lead in retention, we reinforce a culture where individuals feel seen, supported, and valued. You can do the same.

TAKEAWAYS

The paradox of power is that it grows when you give it away. By empowering others, leaders create a ripple effect of growth, trust, and success. Sharing power doesn't diminish your influence—it amplifies it by building stronger teams and fostering a culture of accountability and innovation.

As you know, I've seen this firsthand in profound business improvements that resulted from embracing empowerment. By delegating key responsibilities, my team not only landed more new accounts in a single year than ever before but also came together in a unified effort that strengthened relationships and morale across the board.

Empowerment is the ultimate act of leadership. It requires trust, courage, and humility to share power, but the rewards are immeasurable. When you give power away, you don't lose it—you expand it. You create a legacy of leaders who embody the values, vision, and impact you've set in motion. Empowerment isn't just a strategy; it's a philosophy that transforms individuals, teams, and organizations.

If holding on to control has left you overwhelmed and exhausted, it's time to let go. Real strength isn't in doing everything yourself—it's in building a team that thrives even when you're not in the room. By embracing the paradox of shared power, you'll uncover the true strength of leadership: enabling others to succeed and grow while driving exceptional results.

PARADOX 7

VULNERABILITIES ARE YOUR SUPERPOWERS

We've talked about a lot of fundamental truths that can elevate your leadership, and paradox 7—the paradox that says your vulnerabilities are your superpowers—is no different.

Many people believe showing vulnerability makes them look weak, exposed, or unworthy of being leaders. They believe that if they show uncertainty, admit mistakes, or express personal challenges, others will see them as less capable, less qualified, or less in control. And so they bottle up struggles, put on a mask, and end up feeling like they're always performing. This leads to exhaustion, loneliness, and a lack of real trust with others.

If you've felt like this, I have good news for you: The reality is the opposite. Vulnerability, when used wisely, creates trust. It is an act of humility that allows people to see that you are human, real, and someone they can relate to. Hardly a weakness, vulnerability breaks down walls and removes the fear of judgment. It fosters an environment in which others feel safe to be honest, take risks, and grow.

The alternative—hiding vulnerability entirely—has real consequences. Leaders who refuse to show vulnerability can come across as detached, unapproachable, or even intimidating. Their teams hesitate to speak up, admit mistakes, or share ideas because they don't feel safe doing so. Instead of inspiring confidence, they create a culture of guardedness and fear.

A great example of this is something that happened with my kids during my divorce. When a family breaks apart, there's this terrible moment when the safe "team" you've always had feels fractured. I wanted my kids to see me as a good man—someone they loved, felt comfortable around, and could still look up to. Even in the middle of all that pain, I held on to the hope that they'd always know they were loved and that I was still worthy of their trust.

One night, a few years after my divorce, I was in agony. I had a migraine I couldn't shake. I asked my two eldest kids to stay in my room with me. I ended up lying on the hardwood floor because the pain was so intense. As I lay there, I started telling them how much I loved them and how proud I was of them, but the headache only got worse. Then, all of a sudden, I blurted out something I was deeply disappointed in myself for. The floodgates opened. I started telling them things I was ashamed of, mistakes I regretted, ways I felt I had failed, especially how I felt I had failed them.

They didn't pull away; they pulled closer. They lay on my chest, one on each side, my arms around them, crying with me. We were just three broken hearts finding safety in the middle of the hurt. By the time I finished, my headache was gone and so was an invisible wall I hadn't even realized was there.

They kissed me, squeezed me, and told me they loved me. In that moment, we made a deeper connection, the kind that happens only when you stop pretending to be flawless. Vulnerability didn't make them think less of me. It freed us all from the fear of wondering if we were still loved.

While it might not have been a traditional "leadership" moment, that night taught me something I'll never forget: When you have the courage to share your mess, you give people permission to love the real you.

Help people love who you really are, not the image you project. If you do, I think you'll find that your personal and professional lives will change in ways you could never have imagined.

Vulnerability invites connection. It allows leaders to break down walls, admit imperfection, and create a safe space where everyone feels valued. This openness builds a foundation of trust that strengthens teams, drives innovation, and fosters resilience. Vulnerability, anchored by confidence and conviction, ensures clear direction.

The benefits don't end there. Healthy conflict, open disagreements, and spirited debates are essential for strong teams. Vulnerability creates the safety needed for people to challenge ideas, surface concerns, and strengthen solutions without fear. Without it, disagreements stay hidden and quietly erode trust, innovation, and momentum.

Appropriate moments of vulnerability create authentic loyalty, engagement, and trust.

However, it's important to point out here that vulnerability can be exploited or misused. Misused vulnerability usually shows up as oversharing or as victimhood that seeks sympathy instead of connection. These foster doubt and weaken people's confidence in your leadership.

So when you start to embrace your vulnerability, keep in mind that the idea isn't to overshare or spill every raw thought. And you certainly shouldn't use it constantly; there is a time and place for it (we'll discuss this more in section 7.3). Like any true superpower, vulnerability must be used with discernment. It works best when it's timely, relevant, and balanced with strength. Share enough to build trust, but hold back enough to protect clarity and confidence, so people connect with the real you and still feel secure in your leadership.

In this paradox, we will explore how wise, honest vulnerability transforms leadership. Through personal stories and practical insights, you'll learn how to embrace vulnerability as a tool for connection and growth. By the end of this paradox, you'll understand how to wield your vulnerability as a superpower—one that inspires and empowers those around you, fostering a culture of trust, innovation, and genuine relationships.

7.1. THE COURAGE TO BE SEEN

Vulnerability begins with the courage to be seen as you truly are. For leaders, this often feels counterintuitive. Many believe they must project strength, confidence, and certainty at all times. Yet the most impactful leaders understand that admitting imperfection doesn't diminish their authority; it amplifies their humanity. "Let your kids catch you talking positively about them" is an important insight every parent should learn. So should managers.

A lesson from my own journey demonstrates this perfectly. You already know that growing up, I lived in homes that weren't my own. I became hyper-observant, constantly reading reactions just to survive. And I noticed something: A lot of women in my family would do everything in their power to always be right. It seemed like being wrong threatened their very worth as people. Back then, I couldn't name it as insecurity; I just felt it.

Disagreeing with one of them in particular was difficult. Blowups would happen...big, loud reactions over things that didn't deserve it, and then that person would twist what happened and share that misinformation with people I loved. It hurt, but what hurt most wasn't the misplaced anger—it was the lack of acknowledgment afterward for the pain they caused. I was yelled at, spoken ill of, and then they'd move on like nothing happened, never apologizing for their behavior. I felt unvalued. I came away from those interactions frustrated, grew numb, and eventually—in order to survive—slipped into going along to get along.

Over time, I stopped being me. I became a people pleaser, losing my edge and confidence. It took decades to reclaim myself—and it started with being willing to be seen as I truly am. I had to be vulnerable to myself, to allow myself to be seen by myself. This was something buried deep inside of me that I just lived around, as if it was a part of me, and I was fine with leaving it there.

But that wasn't sustainable. I needed to learn to be *me*. I've learned that our hurt can make us act out of character toward others. But it can also do internal damage. I am not a people pleaser, but that buried hurt inside of me shrank me down into being a smaller version of myself. Grace and understanding, on the other hand, allow people to grow without losing who they are. Give yourself both of them.

This was a personal example, but the same thing holds true in professional situations. Being seen isn't about exposing every vulnerability; it's about being honest in the moments that matter. Leaders who model this grace and restraint build trust and create an environment in which teams feel safe to take risks, share ideas, and grow together. This environment is where true innovation and loyalty are born.

Vulnerability isn't a weakness—it's the courage to decide as your true self, even when it feels risky. The best leaders don't hide their imperfections; they own them. They model a strength that invites others to be real. This is where trust takes root, where teams dare to innovate, and where your leadership becomes a force that lifts everyone higher.

So embrace your vulnerability. Lead as the real you. After all, that is where your real strength lies.

7.2. STRENGTH IN OPENNESS

Being open in your vulnerability is not just about sharing your struggles; it's about using them to connect with and inspire the people around you. Leaders who embrace vulnerability create deeper, more authentic relationships with their teams, clients, and peers. This openness fosters trust, loyalty, and collaboration.

True openness begins with the courage to be seen for who you really are. It comes from recognizing that you matter. Many leaders focus solely on results or their teams, often overlooking their own value. As leaders, it's essential to balance this drive with authenticity.

Here's the thing: We are more than a collection of people's interpretations or judgments, and when we prioritize being authentically ourselves, we inspire others to do the same.

Here are a few ways to prioritize being your authentic self:

- **Hold vulnerability meetings**: Schedule regular sessions where both you and your team members can share personal or professional challenges in a safe space. This could be part of team-building exercises or leadership development programs where vulnerability is seen as a strength, not a weakness.

- **Ask for help publicly**: When facing a challenge, publicly ask for help from your team. This not only models vulnerability but also sets a precedent for collective problem-solving, enhancing team cohesion and individual empowerment.

- **Create a feedback culture**: Encourage a culture where feedback is given with vulnerability at its core—acknowledging one's own limitations while offering constructive criticism. This can be practiced through peer-feedback sessions where everyone shares what they've learned from their mistakes.

- **Utilize storytelling for connection**: Use storytelling in leadership communications to share personal experiences of failure, learning, and growth. This practice can humanize leadership, making it more relatable and fostering a culture where everyone feels they can learn from their own stories.

As you learn to prioritize being authentic, you'll be better equipped to embrace openness. However, if that seems difficult, there are some simple strategies you can implement to lean more into being open. One powerful way to do this is by being intentional in the words you choose. A simple statement like, "I am in a tough spot and could really use your help," carries incredible weight. It's an honor when someone asks for help, because it's a way of saying, "I'm not sure if I can do this without you." Plus, it forces you (as the one doing the asking) to see the good in others—their skills, abilities, and capacity. More importantly, it gives the other person the ability to make a difference, which is one of the most beautiful things we can do in life. I've made such a difference to others and have had such a difference made in my life by others, and I'm guessing you have too.

A powerful story that illustrates the power of asking for help is this: My business was facing a huge opportunity to grow and expand by acquiring another company. I started learning about the private equity side of our industry and saw how we could build something really strong by merging with other companies with Resicom as the platform. To do this well, I needed to move most day-to-day management tasks off my plate so I could lead the charge on the merger. I was willing, but I knew it would challenge me professionally in ways I hadn't faced before.

At the same time, I was a full-time dad for nearly half the workweek. It was not exactly a recipe for being wildly productive and effective.

Instead of pretending everything was fine, I shared my struggles with my leadership team. I explained how I was working to set better boundaries and prioritize what mattered most. This honesty resonated deeply with my team, many of whom were navigating similar challenges. It sparked conversations about work–life balance and led to company-wide initiatives to support employee well-being, creating an environment in which vulnerability was met with support, not judgment. The moral here: Showing up real doesn't weaken leadership; it deepens it.

Strength in openness means inviting others to be part of the solution. Those moments of shared responsibility foster deeper connections, cultivating a culture of authenticity and trust that empowers everyone to thrive.

7.3. BALANCING VULNERABILITY AND AUTHORITY

While vulnerability is a powerful tool, it must be balanced with authority. Leaders who share too much or appear indecisive risk undermining their credibility. The key is to use vulnerability strategically, sharing enough to build trust while maintaining the confidence and clarity needed to lead.

For example, during a major organizational shift, I faced pushback from some team members who were hesitant about the changes. I acknowledged their concerns and shared my own uncertainties about the transition. However, I also emphasized the vision and the steps we were taking to ensure success. By balancing vulnerability with authority, I demonstrated empathy without wavering in my commitment to the company's goals.

This balance is crucial in leadership. Vulnerability without authority can seem directionless, while authority without vulnerability can feel cold and disconnected. Leaders who master this balance create teams that trust their vision and feel empowered to contribute to its success.

Share the "why" behind your decisions while admitting when you're unsure. This transparency can be practiced in decision-making meetings where you outline your thought process, including your doubts, to model balanced leadership. Consider having "vulnerability check-ins" too: Before making significant decisions, set aside time to check in with your team. Ask for their insights, share your concerns, and then make a decision—that is the key to allowing both vulnerability and authority to play roles in your leadership.

Finally, as we discussed previously, delegate tasks in a way that shows trust in your team's capabilities, explaining why you believe they are the right people for the job and how your own limitations led to this decision.

7.4. AVOIDING CONFLICT DOESN'T PREVENT IT— IT BURIES IT DEEPER

"There are too many conversations about John, without John." I've said this more times than I'd like. It's a simple way to call out something deeply frustrating—the feeling of knowing people have formed opinions about you without ever bringing their concerns to you directly. That's not healthy conflict—that's gossipy conflict, and it corrodes trust like rust on steel.

The real issue isn't disagreement. It's avoidance. People sidestep hard conversations, thinking they're keeping the peace, but in reality, they're just letting silence do the damage for them.

The solution? Lead with vulnerability. Instead of accusations, start with how you feel: "I feel blindsided when conversations *about* me happen *without* me." This forces clarity—either the other person realizes they've been feeding the wrong kind of conflict and course-corrects, or they dig their heels in, revealing a deeper issue that needs attention. Either way, you're no longer in the dark. (A tip here: Some conversations need to be had directly, while others are best handled through the right person. If history, hierarchy, or emotional baggage clouds the discussion, empower someone else to carry the message effectively.)

If being direct like this makes you uncomfortable, consider this: Conflict itself isn't the enemy—healthy conflict is a good and necessary force. Tough conversations push teams to grow, expose problems that need fixing, and clear the air before resentment festers. But when conflict turns into gossip, passive-aggressiveness, or back-channeling, it no longer drives progress; it feeds toxicity. Unspoken frustrations don't dissolve; they spread like mold. To be an effective and extraordinary leader, you must create a culture where issues are addressed openly, not in whispers.

I had the opportunity to do this with one of my team members at Resicom. She was someone I worked closely with—someone who, on the surface, always acted like she had my back, nodding in agreement and telling me what she thought I wanted to hear. But behind closed doors, she told a different story to others, stirring confusion and doubt. That's one of the quickest ways to poison trust on any team.

In reflecting on how to handle it, I decided to first see if there was a way to get her to correct her own behavior. Our management team isn't just a top-down chain of command. It's more like a circle of peers who hold each other accountable and lean on each other for support. So before I stepped in, I asked a few team members to help her get back on track. When those efforts didn't work and she didn't self-correct, I knew it was time for a direct conversation.

I sat her down and told her plainly she could not separate herself from her responsibilities when things went wrong. I reminded her that trust is built when you stand with your team, not when you deflect and blame others. I made sure she heard both my belief in her and my expectations for real change. I was surprised when her behavior didn't improve—her fear clearly ran deeper than any conversation with me could fix. But having that hard talk out in the open revealed the real issue: She wasn't in the right position, at least at that point in time. Avoiding that conflict would have only buried the problem until it spread even further.

When you lead with your true self, tough decisions spark healthy conflict that strengthens teams instead of corrosive whispers that tear them apart. Conflict handled well builds trust and momentum. Gossip-driven conflict erodes both. The choice isn't between conflict or no conflict—the choice is between healthy, direct conversations or corrosive, behind-the-scenes destruction. The best leaders don't let silence or avoidance drive the conversation for them—they step into the moment and shape it with intention.

Deal with conflict directly or it will deal with you.

TAKEAWAYS

Vulnerability is not a weakness; it is a superpower. Leaders who embrace their humanity build trust, deepen connections, and inspire others to lead with authenticity. By showing the courage to be seen, finding strength in openness, and balancing vulnerability with authority, you can create a culture where every individual feels valued, heard, and supported. This is not just about leadership; it's about fostering an environment in which everyone is free to grow, innovate, and contribute from their true selves.

By embracing your vulnerability, you will unlock your potential to lead with authenticity. In doing so, you not only inspire those around you to do the same but also cultivate a leadership style that resonates with the core of human experience—connection, growth, and mutual respect.

If you've ever felt the pressure to hide your struggles out of fear of judgment, know this: Your greatest influence will come not from pretending to have it all together but from showing others that strength and imperfection can coexist.

Remember, the true measure of leadership isn't just in achieving goals but in how you bring others along, creating a legacy of empowerment and empathy.

PARADOX 8

YOUR RIGHT ANSWERS ARE DIFFERENT THAN MINE

Running a business is hard. The decisions we make as leaders can mean the difference between a business that thrives and one that doesn't. Couple that fact with all the advice that's out there—advice that tells us to do what worked for someone else—and it's tempting to try to copy what other people are doing.

The reality is that we waste so much time trying to run someone else's plays. People spend years chasing others' success, copying their solutions, only to end up exhausted, disappointed, and doubting themselves. It's like having the solution in your hands but searching desperately for a problem to fit it.

Someone else's path always seems like the proven way forward. After all, their strategy worked (for their skills, timing, and circumstances). But here's the paradox: What is right for them may be completely wrong for you.

The most effective answers aren't found in copying others or chasing popular wisdom. They are discovered by understanding and honoring your distinct identity. Your right answers aren't just different from someone else's; they are uniquely yours, shaped by the mosaic of your experiences, aspirations, and gifts.

True leadership doesn't come from imitation or crowd approval. It comes from building a life and leadership framework that fits *you*—your strengths, your values, and your vision. This alignment creates the confidence to lead authentically and inspire others to do the same.

Every person is a masterpiece, crafted by God with intentionality. Just as we long to be seen and valued for who we are, we are called to extend that same grace to others. The commandment to "love your neighbor as yourself" (Matthew 22:39) reminds us that the care we take in honoring our own uniqueness should mirror how we uplift others. By celebrating their distinctiveness, we foster a world where collaboration thrives, trust deepens, and everyone shines as they were created to.

We are each intentionally uniquely made. Friendships, marriages, and teams all flourish through different dynamics, not sameness. What brings one person joy might not resonate with another. That's not a flaw. Success isn't about fitting into someone else's mold. It's about embracing the gifts and desires placed within you. Being yourself isn't selfish; it's a service to others, allowing the right relationships, opportunities, and missions to find you.

When you live as your true self, you become a great teammate, a trusted leader, and a force for good. You make decisions that align with your heart. You build a life worth living.

At its heart, this paradox teaches us that knowing yourself is essential. When you are clear about who you are and what drives you, you lead with courage, foster trust, and spark innovation. You don't just find better solutions—you build better connections, stronger organizations, and a deeper sense of purpose.

By the end of this paradox, you'll learn how to trust your judgment, define success on your terms, and lead from a place of authenticity and strength. Because at the end of the day, your right answers will always be different than mine—and that's exactly the way it's meant to be.

Be you.

8.1. UNDERSTANDING YOURSELF FIRST

To find *your* right answers, begin with the most fundamental questions about who you are. What is your definition of a good person? This question isn't just about moral philosophy; it's the foundation of how you approach every decision. When your actions align with this definition, they create a confidence that fuels progress. This becomes part of your leadership manifesto (which we'll explore more in the next section)—a tool that simplifies decision-making and ensures you remain true to yourself, even when faced with complexity.

I learned early in my career that emulating others doesn't lead to success. I can still remember how much I admired another leader whose approach was highly effective—for him. But when I tried to replicate his style, I struggled. My team felt disconnected, and I constantly second-guessed my choices. It wasn't until I paused to reflect on my own strengths (and put those reflections into practice) that I began to thrive. I realized that my ability to listen deeply, communicate clearly, and foster collaboration were my greatest assets. When I leaned into these qualities, my leadership transformed. This realization reminds me of a lesson I often share: "If I ran Michael Jordan's plays, we would lose every game." His plays were designed for his unique skills and strengths. Or imagine if Michael Jordan were to attempt to run Shaquille O'Neal's plays. It simply wouldn't work. The same applies to leadership. Your path to success is built on your individual abilities and circumstances. By understanding your own "playbook," you can lead with clarity and authenticity.

This is why taking time to understand yourself isn't just helpful—it's essential. Understanding our unique definitions of a "good person" gives us incredible insight into who we are. In the Be You! Manifesto™ workbook (which we'll go through in the next section), you'll gather insights from three powerful angles: your own perspective, how others see you, and independent assessments that bring surprising clarity about yourself. After all, when we understand ourselves first, we're better able to see where we naturally connect—to situations, to people, and to opportunities. Just as importantly, we learn what to disconnect from.

Going through this workbook myself helped me realize some really neat things about myself—like how much stronger I am when my closest team gives me the benefit of the doubt. I had never realized it before. That kind of trust fuels my confidence and effectiveness. In contrast, others on my team feel strongest when there are diverse opinions in the room, sharpening their ideas. It's really amazing how uniquely made each of us is.

When we encourage each other to be ourselves, we naturally find the places, people, and missions we are meant to connect with. We live and lead much more fully, and we help others do the same.

8.2. YOUR LIFE, YOUR DECISIONS

In leadership, authenticity is a superpower. It's something no one can replicate. Authentic leaders stand out because they are rooted in their strengths, values, and unique perspectives.

The Parable of the Talents illustrates that success is deeply personal and rooted in faithful action, not comparison. In the story, a master entrusts different amounts of money to three servants, rewarding them not based on how much they produce, but how wisely they use what they were given. The master celebrates both the servant who doubled five talents and the one who doubled two equally, showing that success isn't about matching outcomes—it's about using your gifts fully and courageously.

The third servant is criticized for burying his talent. When the servant protests, the master doesn't argue—he calls him lazy for failing to act in accordance with his own beliefs. This is an important nuance that gets overlooked—this servant's "right answer" could have been as simple as earning modest interest by placing the talent in the bank. His mistake is in failing to align his actions with his beliefs, revealing that leadership requires both courage and accountability.

Two servants in the Parable of the Talents, then, succeed by acting within their capacity. Even the third servant is given a pathway to success that matches his ability. As it is in the parable, so it is in life: Strong and effective leadership requires recognizing that the right solutions differ based on individual and team capacities.

Life is full of so many priorities, yet people often focus on the ones that are most visible. True fulfillment often comes from areas the world overlooks. The Parable of the Talents reminds us that success shouldn't be measured by comparing outcomes—it should be measured by how faithfully we invest what we've been given. And so, if you ever feel like you're accomplishing less than someone else, try something different: Appreciate their success without rating yourself against it. Let it inspire you rather than diminish you.

Remember, comparison kills joy. When you catch yourself comparing, pause and name what you admire about the other person's result and the effort it took to achieve it. This helps you see the work behind their success, so you can focus on your own path instead of their outcome. It also humanizes them and gives you something real to compliment—turning comparison into genuine appreciation.

One man I know never accumulated wealth, but he built a family so extraordinary that even his wealthiest peers admired (and maybe even envied) him. Success in life shouldn't be measured by the common scoreboards. Instead, like the Parable of the Talents calls us to do, act faithfully with what you've been given, trust your unique path, and celebrate the differences that make each of us essential contributors.

8.3. DIFFERENTIATING THROUGH STRENGTHS

One of the greatest lessons I've learned is that leadership isn't about universal truths; it's about understanding yourself and leading from that place. Forgiveness, for example, is one of my gifts. It shapes how I approach challenges. For someone else, self-preservation might be their right answer, shaped by their experiences. Both are valid as long as they align with the individual's strengths and context.

During a pivotal moment in my career, a client questioned the value my company brought. Instead of mimicking competitors, I leaned into what made us different: tailored solutions, transparent communication, and long-term relationships. This authenticity not only helped us retain the client but also deepened our partnership.

This goes hand in hand with paradox 6. Since that pivotal moment, I've understood that knowing my strengths also means recognizing when others are better equipped. Sometimes it's teammates junior to me who handle challenges with more patience or connection than I could. Trusting their strengths has consistently allowed our team to succeed where my way would have fallen short. Leaders don't need to be the strongest in every area. They are stronger when they build a team where everyone's authentic strengths are put to work.

Encourage authenticity within your team. Create an environment in which individuality is celebrated, and strengths are embraced. For instance, we have a team member who excels at creating a positive atmosphere. Recognizing this, we let him organize biweekly themed lunches, turning his talent for fostering connection into a valuable asset for office culture.

When you lead this way, you embrace your own "right answers." At the same time, you help people become the best versions of themselves by giving them space to find *their* right answers. And that's the kind of leadership that changes everything.

TAKEAWAYS

The most impactful leaders trust themselves to create their own path, understanding that their right answers are different from anyone else's. Leadership is not about imitation; it's about alignment—with your strengths, your team's capacities, and your vision.

Authenticity, humility, and mutual respect are qualities that drive fulfillment and meaningful leadership. When people understand that their "right answers" are unique, they stop measuring themselves against others and begin to trust their own abilities and experiences. This self-awareness not only builds confidence but also helps individuals align their actions with their values, creating a sense of purpose and clarity in their decisions.

Moreover, recognizing that others have different "right answers" encourages empathy and interdependence. It shifts focus from competition to collaboration, where diverse strengths are celebrated rather than compared. This perspective helps build stronger teams, deeper relationships, and communities that thrive on mutual respect and shared purpose.

For too long, you may have sought validation in someone else's path, believing their answers held the key to your success. But your greatest impact will come when you stop chasing someone else's version of success and fully own your own.

The world needs authentic contributions, not homogenized, copy-paste versions of someone else's life. Trust that who you are is exactly what's needed. Lead boldly from the life you were made to live. By embracing this paradox, you unlock your potential, inspire others to do the same, and help create a more connected and harmonious world.

I've said it before, but it bears repeating: **Be you!**

WRAP-UP

THE 8 PARADOXES

LEADERSHIP ISN'T ABOUT FINDING THE *RIGHT* ANSWERS—it's about discovering *your* answers. Throughout this book, we've explored paradoxes that challenge conventional wisdom: how boundaries create freedom, how failure fuels success, how power grows when you give it away, and others. Each paradox reveals a deeper truth: Effective leadership isn't about fitting into a mold, but about building a framework that aligns with who you are. When you lead from authenticity, clarity, and confidence, you unlock not only your own potential but also the potential of those around you.

The Be You! Manifesto™, which we'll examine next, is your personal compass—a declaration of how you will lead, what you stand for, and what you refuse to compromise. It is a tool for clarity, a guide for decision-making, and a reminder of the type of leader you aspire to be. More than that, it gives you a structure to return to when challenges arise.

Before we go on, I want to leave you with one final point: Leadership isn't just about you—it's about the impact you have on others. The strongest leaders are those who empower, trust, and invest in their teams. They don't hoard power; they share it. They don't fear vulnerability; they embrace it as a source of connection and strength. And most importantly, they understand that accountability isn't about restriction—it's about liberation.

When you build a culture of trust and responsibility, you create an environment in which creativity thrives, risks lead to rewards, and people bring their best selves to the table. The path forward won't always be clear, but that's the nature of leadership. So as you work through the Be You! Manifesto™, remember: You don't need certainty to move forward—you just need conviction.

PART 2

OVERVIEW TO THE BE YOU! MANIFESTO™

Now that we've gone through the 8 Paradoxes, it's time to take the next step: exploring a framework that will help articulate your core identity and definition of a good person. This is the key to turning you into the extraordinary leader that you are.

I wasted years feeling misunderstood, drained by expectations, and overwhelmed by responsibilities that never seemed to let up. I made decisions not because they were right for me, but because I wanted to avoid conflict, avoid being questioned, and avoid being misinterpreted. I was exhausted—professionally, emotionally, and mentally—believing the problem was with the world I found myself in. And then, I had an epiphany: I realized the problem wasn't the world around me. It was that I had no framework for operating in it with clarity and strength.

That's why I created the Be You! Manifesto™—a game changer designed to eliminate unnecessary stress, anxiety, and inefficiency in how we lead, make decisions, and engage with others. This isn't another leadership formula that forces you into someone else's mold. It's a personalized framework that helps you define who you are, build relationships that strengthen rather than drain you, and optimize your energy so you can lead and live at your highest level without burning out. Whether you're leading a team, a company, or simply yourself, this manifesto will give you tools to move with confidence, protect your peace, and take control of your life.

The Be You! Manifesto™ complements the 8 Paradoxes well. The paradoxes offer the foundation for an open mind—and the freedom to challenge ideas that sound good but secretly mislead us. Paradox 8 in particular demonstrates just how important it is to stop filling in someone else's answers for your own life. It reminds us that we can be fully ourselves and feel more complete than if we spend our energy chasing someone else's version of more.

That's the heartbeat behind the Be You! Manifesto™. If the Paradoxes help you see the world and your leadership differently, the Manifesto helps you articulate your core identity so you can live out your difference every day. It gives you a practical, personal operating system to stay clear, focused, and anchored in who you are—especially when life gets messy.

The Be You! Manifesto™ has three key areas:

1. CORE IDENTITY: YOUR DEFINITION OF A GOOD PERSON

Everything begins with defining your **Core Identity**. Without understanding that, you'll live on autopilot—reacting to life's challenges instead of shaping them. Most people never take the time to truly define who they are, what they believe in, and what they stand for. Instead, they drift, constantly second-guessing themselves, making choices that satisfy external pressures instead of aligning with their deeper truth. The result? Stress, self-doubt, and an underlying sense of dissatisfaction, no matter how much they achieve.

The Manifesto starts by helping you craft a clear definition of what it means to be a good person—on your terms. It challenges you to establish your core values and virtues, explore personality profiles to understand your natural strengths, and articulate your long-term vision. You will build your own Authenticity Reminders—mental anchors that keep you aligned with your identity in moments of doubt. Without this clarity, you will always be pulled in different directions, constantly questioning whether you're on the right path. With it, though, you become unshakable—capable of making decisions with conviction, knowing exactly who you are and what you stand for.

When you understand yourself and have a well-defined Core Identity, you are your most powerful. You stop making decisions based on fear or societal pressure, and you start leading from a place of strength. You stop wasting energy questioning yourself, and instead, you direct that energy toward building the life, relationships, and career that truly align with who you are. With a rock-solid Core Identity, every decision, every challenge, and every opportunity becomes clearer, simpler, and more aligned with your highest potential.

2. BOUNDARIES AND RELATIONSHIPS: INTERACTING WELL

The second key area of the Manifesto deals with Boundaries and Relationships. Most stress in leadership and life doesn't come from the work itself—it comes from people. It comes from misunderstandings, unclear expectations, and the exhaustion of constantly managing others' needs while neglecting your own. Leaders and high achievers often struggle to set boundaries, fearing they will appear selfish, unapproachable, or difficult. But without clear boundaries, you become a prisoner to others' expectations, sacrificing your well-being for the sake of keeping the peace.

Boundaries are not walls—they are road maps for how people engage with you. They tell others what you will and will not tolerate, how you prefer to communicate, and where your limits are. Strong boundaries eliminate the chaos of miscommunication, prevent unnecessary conflicts, and allow you to protect your focus for what truly matters. The Be You! Manifesto™ helps you build a Manifesto Lite for boundaries, use the MyOS™ Trust & Apology Framework for relationships, and utilize the BUILD method to navigate difficult conversations—ensuring that your relationships become sources of strength rather than stress.

When you master this area of the Manifesto, you no longer waste time explaining yourself, justifying your decisions, or managing other people's emotions at your own expense. You gain the power to focus on what moves the needle in your life, knowing that your relationships are aligned, your interactions are clear, and your personal space is respected. With strong boundaries, you stop being drained by others and start leading with clarity, confidence, and balance.

3. ENERGY MANAGEMENT: FORTITUDE

The final key area of the Be You! Manifesto™ is energy management.

Most people don't lack time—they lack energy. They spend their days caught in low-value tasks, reactive decisions, and distractions that drain them mentally, physically, and emotionally. By the time they get to the work that actually matters, they're too exhausted to bring their best self to it. The Be You! Manifesto™ ensures that you master energy management, allowing you to operate at peak performance without running yourself into the ground.

The Manifesto helps you conduct an Energy Audit to identify what fuels you and what drains you. You'll develop a To-Don't List, removing tasks and obligations that sap your focus. You'll also go through an exercise to ensure that your efforts are spent on what actually moves the needle, not just on what feels urgent. Leaders who fail at energy management often burn out, make short-sighted decisions, and struggle to sustain high performance over time. This part gives you the tools to avoid that fate—to sustain long-term success without sacrificing your well-being.

Energy management is about more than productivity—it's about being intentional with your effort, protecting your mental clarity, and ensuring that every day you wake up with the capacity to lead powerfully. That way, you can build momentum and make sure you focus only on what matters, eliminate what doesn't, and operate with a level of clarity and stamina that others can't match.

When you control your energy, you control everything.

WORKSHEETS

This section will take you through a series of exercises to help you develop your personal Be You! Manifesto™. They are designed to bring clarity to who you are, what you stand for, and how you operate at your best.

At the end of each worksheet (where applicable), I've added my own answers. These are intended to serve as an example in case you need some inspiration. Remember paradox 8, though: Your right answers are different than mine. I've included my answers simply as examples, but feel free to disregard them if you think they'll sway your own responses.

One more note before we dive in: Avoid the temptation to make your answers perfect. Consider each exercise a draft until the very end. The goal is not perfection—it's progress. Each worksheet reveals a bit more about you, helping you refine and sharpen your leadership framework. By the time you complete them all, you will have revised, adjusted, and strengthened your Manifesto in ways you couldn't have anticipated at the start.

Visit *www.johnfairclough.com/book-resources* to access worksheets and more resources.

WORKSHEET 1
DEFINING YOUR CORE VALUES AND CORE VIRTUES

Core values and core virtues are the foundation of your Core Identity—shaping how you lead, live, and align with your authentic self. Together, they form the bedrock of your Be You! Manifesto™, giving you clarity, confidence, and consistency in how you move through life. While they are deeply connected, they serve distinct roles:

- **Core values = How you act**
    - These define your external behavior—how you show up in relationships, work, and leadership.
    - They guide your priorities, decisions, and expectations for yourself and others.

- **Core virtues = Who you are**
    - These define your internal character—the moral qualities that anchor you.
    - They shape how you navigate challenges, maintain integrity, and handle adversity.

If core values are the compass that directs your decisions, core virtues are the foundation that keeps you standing strong. This worksheet helps you reveal—not create—your values and virtues, which are already present in your reactions, experiences, and beliefs. By the end, you'll have a clear framework to guide your decisions, strengthen your confidence, and establish your personal definition of a good person. (Remember, I've added my own answers at the end of the worksheet as an example.)

STEP ONE: UNDERSTAND THE DIFFERENCE

Before diving in, let's clarify how core values and core virtues differ and work together:

	Core Values	Core Virtues
Focus	How you act in the world.	Who you are inside.
Source	Revealed through what you admire or dislike in others.	Revealed through your proudest and most regretful moments.
Purpose	Shape how you interact, lead, and make decisions.	Ensure your integrity, resilience, and moral strength.
Example	If you value reliability, you expect people to follow through.	If you embody courage, you take action even when afraid.

A value like "reliability" might drive you to keep promises, while a virtue like "integrity" ensures you do so even when it's hard. Together, they define a person who acts consistently and stands firm.

STEP TWO: UNCOVER YOUR CORE VALUES (HOW YOU ACT)

Core values aren't invented—they're revealed through your emotional reactions to people and situations. This step will help you articulate the principles that matter most to you.

1. **Make a Love List**
   - List five to seven behaviors you admire in others (at work, in leadership, in life).
   - Why does each one matter to you?
   - Example: "I love when people are punctual because it shows respect for my time."

2. **Make a Hate List**
   - List five to seven behaviors that frustrate you in others.
   - Why do these behaviors bother you?
   - Example: "I hate when people lie because it breaks my trust."

3. **Flip It**
   - For each behavior on your hate list, flip it to its positive opposite—these are often your true values.
   - Example: "dishonesty" flips to "honesty."

4. **Craft Your Core Values**
   - Combine your love and flipped-hate list and distill it down to your strongest three to five values. (I have four core values.)
   - Write one sentence explaining why each value matters to you.
   - Example: "Reliability: I prioritize being someone others can count on because inconsistency wastes everyone's energy."

5. **Integrate into Your Be You! Manifesto™**
   - Add these values under "How I Act (core values)" in your Be You! Manifesto™.
   - Once you add them, do a quick pulse check and see if you can identify recent decisions you've made that line up with the values, and others that violate them. This will become part of your "Weekly 1-on-1" meeting with yourself that you'll build later.

STEP THREE: DISCOVER YOUR CORE VIRTUES (WHO YOU ARE)

Core virtues are the moral qualities that define your character—what remains constant in success, failure, hardship, and growth.

- **List initial virtues.** Write down four to six virtues you aspire to embody (e.g., integrity, courage, patience, humility).
- **Reflect on a proud moment.** Think of a time you faced a challenge and were proud of how you handled it. What virtues were at play?
- **Reflect on a regretful moment.** Think of a time when you didn't act as your best self. What virtues were missing?
- **Refine your core virtues.** Based on these reflections, finalize your four to five most defining virtues. Write one sentence for each explaining how it shapes your life.
- **Integrate into your Be You! Manifesto™.** Add these virtues under "Who I Am (core virtues)."
- **Use them as a personal compass.** In tough situations, ask: Am I acting in alignment with my virtues?

• • •

JOHN'S MANIFESTO EXAMPLE

My Core Values

- **Honor the Promise.** Commitments matter, especially the implied ones. Every person on your team is here for a reason—to make the company better and stronger. That's the unspoken agreement, and it's up to leadership to ensure that promise is fulfilled. Honor extends beyond contracts; it's about taking responsibility for the role you play in relationships, business, and personal growth.
- **Be Courageous.** Take on challenges, expand your comfort zone, and stand firm in your principles. Approaching life's

battles with an open mind is critical to success. Seek out good information, be prudently humble, and resist the temptation to simply "go along to get along." Difficult conversations often build the best relationships—have them.

- **Move Forward**. Progress requires learning and developing your skills, but more importantly, it depends on forgiveness. People will let you down, and you will let yourself down. The ability to forgive, both others and yourself, is essential to advancing. Do it often.

- **Value People**. Everyone has strengths, weaknesses, and personal battles. Whether we like it or not, we need one another. Choosing to see the good in others strengthens both them and us. We have a responsibility to invest in people and foster an environment in which they can thrive.

My Core Virtues

- My core virtue is **Prudence**: I believe it perfects all other virtues. It brings together multiple virtues at one time, and being a problem-solver, I realize that there are lots of ways to see things. I love to bring them together. For example, St. Thomas Aquinas talked about justice and mercy and said something to the effect of "Justice without mercy is cruelty. Mercy without justice is dissolution." Without prudently administering justice, we run the risk of being cruel.

- **Love of God and Neighbor**: Loving God and others is at my core. True love requires action, sacrifice, and honoring dignity. I strive to leave people better than I found them, leading with purpose, humility, and integrity in all relationships.

- **Forgiveness and Mercy**: Forgiveness is a statement of worth, a way of saying, "You are more than your worst moment." I forgive freely—not to excuse, but to release and restore. I see beyond mistakes while maintaining boundaries that protect growth and accountability.

- **Authenticity (Salt of the Earth)**: I was created with unique gifts, weaknesses, and purpose—my calling is to fully embrace and use them. Being authentic means investing my energy wisely, protecting what matters, and inspiring others to do the same.

- **Interpret Well**: How I see the world shapes how I lead. I have to see the good, and I align my focus with God's purpose, and my path becomes clear. I filter out distractions, make wise, intentional decisions, and commit to what truly matters.

WORKSHEET 2
PERSONALITY INSIGHTS

Understanding yourself is the cornerstone of authentic leadership—and personality assessments are your key to unlocking it. These independent profiles, backed by decades of research, reveal your natural strengths, work styles, and behavioral tendencies, cutting through the noise of self-doubt and societal pressure. They don't define you—they illuminate who you already are, stripping away the anxiety of trying to be someone else and replacing it with confidence in being you.

Why use multiple personality assessments? Because each offers a unique lens into how you lead, think, and execute.

These insights help you align with your strengths, ensuring you operate at your highest level in decisions, leadership, and interactions.

STEP ONE: TAKE THREE PERSONALITY ASSESSMENTS

To gain a well-rounded understanding of your natural tendencies, complete these assessments:

- **Omnia Profile**: Measures assertiveness, sociability, pace, and independence.
- **Myers-Briggs (MBTI)**: Identifies your cognitive style based on four dimensions.
- **Working Genius**: Reveals your two strongest areas, showing where you naturally thrive.

There are other tools as well, if you feel drawn to explore further. I know people who love DISC, StrengthsFinder, or Enneagram.

STEP TWO: ANALYZE YOUR RESULTS

Each of these assessments tells you something critical about how you operate in work, leadership, and relationships. Using the questions in the list below as inspiration, identify two to three key takeaways per assessment, then write them down (you can put them in your own words or use the descriptions you get from the assessment).

- **Omnia Profile**: How bold or cautious am I? Do I work better independently or within structure?
- **MBTI**: How do I process information? Do I rely on logic or emotion? Do I work best alone or with others?
- **Working Genius**: Do I thrive in strategy, execution, or somewhere in between?

STEP THREE: SUMMARIZE YOUR FINDINGS

Now, distill your insights into three to five powerful statements that capture how you naturally operate. Write your own statements based on each of your assessments.

Example Personality Statements:

- "I am a bold strategist who thrives on challenge, shaping solutions with precision and confidence."
- "I lead decisively and independently, delegating details so I can focus on vision and impact."
- "I process information analytically, preferring facts first, then evaluation, then action."
- "I innovate and discern—excelling in big-picture thinking but relying on others for execution."

- "I work best when my autonomy is respected and decisions are made with clarity and speed."

STEP FOUR: INTEGRATE INTO YOUR BE YOU! MANIFESTO™

Add these statements under "Personality Insights" in your Be You! Manifesto™.

Remember to own your strengths. These profiles don't just describe you—they equip you. They help you understand yourself.

• • •

JOHN'S MANIFESTO EXAMPLE

Myers–Briggs (MBTI)

I am an INTJ in Myers–Briggs (Mastermind). I am a strategic and decisive leader who thrives on big-picture problem-solving, direct communication, and empowering others to rise, all while moving with focus, efficiency, and conviction.

- **Strategic and Visionary**: Big-picture thinker, thrives on challenge.
- **Independent and Decisive**: Forms own conclusions, trusts own judgment.
- **Action-Oriented and Efficient**: Moves quickly, executes with focus.
- **High Standards and No-Nonsense Communication**: Direct and practical.
- **Empowering Yet Demanding Leader**: Pushes others to rise while providing support.

Omnia Profile

John is a decisive, high-performing leader who operates with clarity, speed, and high expectations. He is self-reliant, solution-focused, and expects those around him to execute at a high level. While deeply loyal to those he trusts, he has low tolerance for inefficiency, indecisiveness, or excuses.

- **Decisive and Goal-Oriented**: John moves with purpose and efficiency, eliminating distractions and focusing on results. He adjusts quickly when something isn't working and expects those around him to do the same. Wasted time and inefficiencies are unacceptable.

- **Independent and Self-Sufficient**: John trusts his own judgment first and operates best with people who take ownership of their work. He values competence and accountability and finds excessive oversight frustrating.

- **High Standards and Strong Expectations**: John expects excellence, accountability, and results. He pushes people to grow and has little patience for excuses. He believes problems should always come with solutions and that people should rise to challenges, not avoid them.

- **Direct and Practical Communicator**: John values clear, efficient, and solution-focused communication. He prefers facts first, then analysis, and dislikes opinions presented as reality. He expects honesty without unnecessary sugarcoating.

- **Fast-Moving and Efficient**: John processes information quickly and expects others to keep pace and execute without hesitation. He has little tolerance for unnecessary deliberation and values people who adapt and move forward effectively.

- **Loyal but Expects Loyalty in Return:** John is deeply loyal to those he trusts and expects the benefit of the doubt in return. His inner circle should ask him for clarity before assuming the worst. He does not tolerate gossip, disloyalty, or passive-aggressiveness, preferring direct and open conversations.

Working Genius

Your areas of Working Genius are **Discernment and Invention (D I)**

- You are naturally gifted at and derive energy and joy from using your intuition and instincts to evaluate and assess ideas or plans.
- You are naturally gifted at and derive energy and joy from creating original and novel ideas and solutions.

Your areas of Working Competency are **Wonder and Enablement (W E)**

- You are capable of and don't mind pondering the possibility of greater potential and opportunity in a given situation.
- You are capable of and don't mind providing others with encouragement and assistance for projects and tasks.

Your areas of Working Frustration are **Galvanizing and Tenacity**.

- You aren't naturally gifted at and don't derive energy and joy from rallying people and inspiring them to take action around ideas, projects, or tasks.
- You aren't naturally gifted at and don't derive energy and joy from pushing projects and tasks through to completion to ensure that the desired results are achieved.

WORKSHEET 3
DEVELOP YOUR DEFINITION OF A GOOD PERSON

A good person isn't molded by fleeting trends or societal checklists—they are forged by the principles they choose to live by. True confidence and leadership emerge from knowing who you are and what you stand for, giving you clarity and purpose to face life's challenges. Without these anchors, you're adrift, reacting to the world instead of shaping it.

This worksheet guides you to craft your definition of a good person—blending your core values, core virtues, and personality insights from Worksheets 1 and 2 with the qualities you admire in others. Remember, this is not about perfection; it's about a standard that's yours alone, a compass for decisions you can stand behind.

By the end of this worksheet, you'll have written a concise, powerful definition of a good person—which you can then turn into your guide to living and leading authentically, which will provide a foundation for unshakable confidence.

1. **Start with a person you admire.** Begin with inspiration. Write down the name of someone you deeply respect—a historical figure, mentor, or personal connection. They don't need to be flawless, just real. List three to five qualities and their guiding principles that make them admirable.

    a. Write a sentence about why each quality resonates with you (one sentence per quality).

    b. Write a sentence about how this person makes you feel.

2. **Examine your core values and core virtues.** Review your core values ("How I Act") and virtues ("Who I Am") from Worksheet 1. Select two to three values and virtues that you see as essential to being a good person.

   a. Write a sentence linking each of these values and virtues to your standard.

3. **Analyze your personality traits.** Your natural wiring shapes how you embody your principles. Reflect on your Personality Insights from Worksheet 2 and write a couple of sentences that summarize some of the distinctive parts of your personality. Add them to your definition.

4. **Refine it into a few paragraphs.** Synthesize your insights into a clear, powerful definition. Blend admiration, core values, core virtues, and traits into a standard that's authentic and actionable. Write your definition, starting with "To me, a good man/woman/person is..." Keep the statement concise, yet meaningful. (See my example at the end of this worksheet.)

5. **Integrate into your Be You! Manifesto™.** Your definition is your compass—embed it in your Be You! Manifesto™ to guide your life and leadership. Add your paragraphs under "Definition of a Good Person" in your Manifesto.

You must make decisions that you are proud of. Without a clear definition, you're at the mercy of the world's shifting tides. This standard—built on admiration, values, virtues, and self-awareness—grounds you in purpose and integrity. It's not just who you are; it's who you're committed to becoming—a declaration that cuts through doubt and fuels authentic leadership.

JOHN'S MANIFESTO EXAMPLE

Definition of a Good Man

To me, a good man makes people feel loved, valued, happy, safe, strong, and empowered.

- **Honorable**: A good man is honorable. He is accountable to do what he believes is right, regardless of external pressures. He desires to be authentically himself and encourages others to do the same. He wants people to be who God made them to be.

- **Courageous**: A good man is courageous. He inspires hope, always. He will challenge authority when needed and does not go along to get along. He faces adversity knowing that God uses our most difficult moments to introduce us to ourselves.

- **Empowering**: A good man empowers. He sees the good in people and challenges and helps them utilize their strengths. He provides appropriate levels of safety and opportunity.

- **Generous**: A good man is generous. He understands we are interdependent, and he will share his blessings and experiences to the point of being vulnerable if that is what is needed.

- **Forgiving**: A good man forgives freely. He believes he will be forgiven the way he forgives. People make mistakes and forgiving them is a way to tell them, "You are worth more than how your action made me feel."

To me, a good man is himself.

WORKSHEET 4

STANDARD BOUNDARIES

The relationships we build—personal, professional, or otherwise—flourish when there's clarity around expectations, tendencies, and limits. We often see boundaries as walls, shutting others out—but that's a myth. Remember paradox 2: Boundaries Build Bridges? Boundaries are road maps, guiding people to engage with you in ways that honor your energy, trust, and purpose. Without them, you're a sponge for others' chaos—frustration festers, misalignment takes root, and burnout drags you from your authentic self into a reactive mess. Clear boundaries aren't selfish; they're vital—they sharpen trust, slash anxiety, and free you to give from strength, not depletion. They're the difference between surviving demands and leading your life.

With that in mind, the exercise we're about to do will help you craft your Standard Boundaries—what I think of as "Warning Labels"—a sharp set of preferences and limits that shows others how you operate best. Pulling from the first three worksheets, you'll define what fuels you, what drains you, and how to sync effectively with others. By the end, you'll have integrated a concise, living framework into your Be You! Manifesto™, enabling you to build stronger relationships, boost teamwork, and protect your purpose.

1. **Define Your Energy Flow.** Energy is your fuel—mastering its flow keeps you sharp and present, not scattered or spent.

    a. Before you start, recall a time you felt fully energized—what sparked it? Now, recall a time you felt drained—what caused it? List two to three energizers and two to three drainers. Then, write a "Respect this by..." statement. *Example: "Respect this by giving me space for deep work—skip the small stuff."*

b. Link it: How does this reflect your Personality Insights (Worksheet 2)? What fuels you? What zaps it? Set your energy boundary and connect it. *Example:* "*My strategic wiring (Personality Insight) thrives on focus, not chatter.*"

2. **Identify Trust Triggers.** Trust holds relationships together—knowing what breaks it keeps you surrounded by the right people.

   a. Before you start, think of a time trust broke—what stung most? List two to three trust breakers. Write a "Preserve this by..." statement.

   b. Link it: How does this tie to your Core Values (Worksheet 1)? What kills your trust? Set your trust boundary and connect it.

3. **Clarify Your Time Needs.** Time is your currency—guarding it keeps you effective and calm, not frazzled.

   a. Before you start, picture your ideal day. When do you shine? When do you fade? Using this insight, list one to two time preferences. Write a "Know this..." statement.

   b. Link it: How does this support your Definition of a Good Person (Worksheet 3)? How do you manage time? Set your time boundary and connect it.

4. **Correct Misunderstandings.** Assumptions muddle connection—clearing them keeps others on your page.

   a. Before you start, recall a time someone misjudged you—what hurt? List one to two misconceptions. Write an "Understand this..." statement.

   b. Link it: How does this reflect your Core Virtues (Worksheet 1)?

5. **Define Your Communication Style.** Communication drives every exchange—nailing it down cuts friction and boosts flow.
   a. Before you start, think of a great conversation that stands out in your mind. What clicked? Then, think of a bad one. What clashed? List your preferred style and one to two frustrations. Write a "Communicate by..." statement.
   b. Link it: How does this align with your Personality Insights? How do you communicate best? Set your communication boundary and connect it.

6. **Integrate and Test Your Warning Label.** Your Warning Label—energy, trust, time, misunderstandings, communication—steers how others sync with you. Add it to your Be You! Manifesto™ to shape your relationships. Place it under "Standard Boundaries."
   a. Test it this week: Where is it working? Where is it challenged? How can you hold firm on it? Refine as it ripples through your Manifesto.

Boundaries don't block—they bond, forging trust and teamwork by aligning others with your true self. And, as we learned in paradox 2, they shield your energy from chaos, cut the anxiety of overstretch, and free you to lead on your terms. Your Warning Label isn't a rule book—it's a living bridge to richer relationships and a life of purpose.

WORKSHEET 5
INSIGHTS FROM OTHERS

Your Core Identity fuses three lenses—your self-view, your assessments, and others' perspectives. This isn't a soft nudge; it's a stark reveal of how you land. Your strengths spark some people, and your edges jar others; bridging that gulf hones your leadership and ties.

To complete this worksheet, seek ten or more people who know you well—colleagues, mentors, peers, friends—and can give you the raw truth. Their "how you make them feel" is your impact's pulse, reflecting the good person you aim to be.

YOUR INSTRUCTIONS

1. **Select the voices.** Choose ten-plus people who actively interact with you.

2. **Gather their take.** Ask for clear input in person or via email or any other way. Here's an example:

   Hi, _____, I need your help. I am creating a quick guide on myself and one of the exercises I have to do is gather other people's feedback. I already did a self-assessment, completed independent assessments, and now I am looking for feedback from people whom I interact with regularly. Please share your thoughts openly. Thank you for your help!

   1. *How do I make you feel?*
   2. *What do you enjoy most about working with or being around me?*
   3. *What three adjectives describe my leadership or communication style?*

4. What challenges or frustrations have you hit with me?
5. What's one thing I could do to lead better?
6. How do you prep for a meeting or talk with me?
7. What advice would you give to someone who wants to start working directly with me?

3. **Map to your Be You! Manifesto**™. Organize the answers you receive so you can populate your Manifesto.
   - Review answers to questions one to three and ensure these words are accurately reflected in your definition of a good person.
   - Review answers to questions four and five and add relevant points to the Things to Consider Working On section.
   - Take the unedited responses to questions two, four, and seven and place them in their appropriate sections of the Manifesto.

By adding others' perspectives to your Be You! Manifesto™, you'll have all three points of view, helping you see yourself more clearly.

• • •

JOHN'S MANIFESTO EXAMPLE

Advice on Working with Me from Direct Reports

- "He challenges you. Every task is a new challenge! I've worked on things here that I never have before at another company."
- "John's leadership style is, hands down, the best I've experienced. He leads by example, never asking anyone to do something he wouldn't do himself."

- "John doesn't just manage people—he develops them. He believes in their potential, pushes them past their limits, and expects them to rise."
- "He's so damn smart that every time he asks me a question, I feel challenged. But in all seriousness, it makes me think differently."
- "John's leadership isn't about control; it's about impact. He sets high standards, but he also invests in people. If you work with him, expect to be challenged and expect to grow."

Quotes About Working with John

- "John has been my biggest cheerleader. He saw potential in me before I saw it in myself and has consistently pushed me to grow, both personally and professionally."
- "John's leadership isn't about authority; it's about impact. He inspires loyalty by being loyal. He motivates others by believing in their potential, even when they don't see it themselves."
- "Working with John is like being handed a front-row seat to a mind that's always racing ahead, ready to change the game. It's about seeing things from a whole new perspective—one you didn't even realize you needed."
- "If a goal isn't met, he'll say, 'No problem' and talk it through to figure out how to get it done and make it successful in the future so we don't hit the same roadblocks. Most people would immediately get mad/upset or beat you up, but John listens and problem-solves."
- "He has challenged me to step into my own—to take accountability not just for my work, but for my team's success

as well. He's never shied away from difficult conversations, but he always delivers them with the intention of helping me become better."

- "He's constantly going a mile a minute. I wish we would fully complete projects/tasks before coming up with new ideas and moving on. He has great ideas and I would like to see them all come to life."

- "John's drive and brilliance make him a powerful force, but not everyone moves at his pace. While he's already ten steps ahead, the rest of us are often still trying to catch up."

- "I wish he would let go a bit more. He's been screwed over in the past, which may be why he holds on so tightly, but trusting his leadership team with more tasks would help lessen the burden of his full plate."

- "We argue about this every time I bring it up, but he changes his mind on decisions quite a bit. Regardless if it's pivoting because things came up or he gets cold feet on a decision, it does happen."

- "John challenges me in ways I didn't even realize I needed. He can sometimes give me tasks that feel nearly impossible. But that's part of his brilliance—he's never interested in easy answers."

WORKSHEET 6
YOUR PRIORITIES

We've already talked about boundaries and delegating in the Paradoxes. And now, we're going to look at something that goes hand in hand with those things: your priorities.

All too often, life's roar—obligations, guilt, endless hum—swamps your voice until priorities fade to frantic static. You mean to hold family, health, or purpose high, but the world's grind—emails, yeses, the fear of no—steals your shot. Businesses wield strategic plans to stay laser-focused, though, so why not you? Research from Daniel Goleman's book *Focus* slams it home: Honed attention cuts distraction by 50 percent, providing you a shield against the chaos.

Drift off track, and the fallout bites—energy bleeds on petty squabbles, frustrations spill onto those you'd rather lift. David Allen's book *Getting Things Done* shows focus isn't just calm—it's your guardrail, slashing stress when priorities rule, not the other way around. This isn't about juggling it all; it's about carving out time for what's of core importance to you—your time and spark are finite, and every yes to noise is a no to your core.

This exercise strips the clutter to bare what's true—not others' checklists, but your fight. It's a reckoning: Where's your energy really going? Goleman calls focus the brain's gatekeeper; Allen ties it to impact—when you track your top priorities, you don't just manage them, you own them. Here in this worksheet, you'll forge a blueprint with intent.

1. **Identify Your Top Priorities**: Top priorities need to be treated as such.
    - Consider your work responsibilities, personal life, family, and anything else that holds deep importance.

- List your three to five most vital priorities.
- For each, answer: Why does this matter to me?
- Add one guiding promise to each of your vital priorities (e.g., "I will be fully present with my family in the evenings.").

2. **Align Your Actions**: Priorities are much more likely to get the attention they deserve when they are reflected in your calendar. Review your priorities and start assigning yourself some time and tasks committed to them. For example, I block out time in my calendar as a meeting with myself.

3. **Audit Last Week**: See where you spent too much time on things that took you away from your priorities unnecessarily.
   - What time did I waste? (Remember downtime is not necessarily wasted time.)
   - Where did I spend too much time on energy-draining items? What impact did that have on my priorities?

4. **The Presence Check**: Even when priorities are clear, are you showing up in the way you intend to? Presence isn't just about time—it's about quality, attention, and engagement.
   - *Action*: For each priority, ask this: Am I proud of the way I am present? If the answer is no, identify one action to correct it.
   - How can I spend just a little more time on what matters most? Commit to this shift.

Naming priorities is the first step. Living them is the real challenge. If you don't protect what matters, the world will bury it under noise. The key to success is managing your priorities with discipline and intention. What gets managed gets done.

WORKSHEET 7
MY RESILIENCE REMINDERS

Failure stings—we're wired to dread it, replay mistakes, and fear judgment. We're told to avoid failure at all costs, yet, as we saw in paradox 4, some of the most powerful breakthroughs—personal and professional—are forged in failure. The problem isn't failure itself; it's how we process it. If we see failure as proof we're not good enough, we shrink. If we recognize it as fuel, we rise.

Research backs this: Carol Dweck's work on growth mindset shows that those who see failure as feedback recover 40 percent faster than those who resist it. Angela Duckworth's writings on grit tie resilience to perseverance—not avoiding failure, but using it. My own experiences support these findings, as I'm guessing yours do too.

However, sometimes remembering to look at failure as feedback can be difficult. Yes, every struggle you've endured has strengthened you—yet in the next storm, those lessons can blur, leaving you doubting your ability to rise again. This exercise, though, has the power to ensure you never forget.

This worksheet helps you extract wisdom from past struggles to create Resilience Reminders—short, fierce truths that anchor you in moments of doubt. This is not about seeking failure but ensuring that when it strikes, you're prepared. Because failure doesn't just happen—it either builds you or breaks you, and you decide which.

1. **Identify your toughest challenges.** Your greatest lessons are buried in your hardest struggles—so dig them up. List three of your most difficult challenges—personal or professional. Next to each, write how it stretched you (e.g., patience, resilience, decision-making).

2. **Extract the lessons.** Every fall hides a lesson—find the gold and master your failures. For each challenge you identified above, answer:

   a. What did I learn about myself?

   b. What strength emerged in that moment (e.g., grit, adaptability, composure)?

3. **Craft your Resilience Reminders.** Transform lessons into battle-tested truths—short, fierce statements to grip when doubt strikes. Write three Resilience Reminders, one per challenge. For example: *"I've rebuilt from the ground up—I'll do it again."*

4. **Integrate and activate.** Resilience isn't theory—it's practice. When the next setback comes, reach for these reminders.

   a. Add them under "Resilience Reminders" in your Manifesto. Read them when adversity strikes.

Remember, your toughest storms didn't break you—they built you. I believe these moments of struggle are when we truly meet ourselves. These reminders are proof: When doubt creeps in, you already have what it takes to rise again

• • •

JOHN'S MANIFESTO EXAMPLE

My Resilience Reminders

- Every challenge makes me stronger—if I let it.
- People are worth more than their mistakes.
- Some people cannot see how great they are.
- "I am here for you" can be more valuable than gold.
- Be you—nobody else can.

Note: Each of these came from one of my toughest challenges. For example, "Every challenge makes me stronger—if I let it" came from my many business challenges, from not having enough money to cover the bills, to not having the right team around me, to clients who owed me a fortune going bankrupt, and so on. Each instance triggered a creative response from me, helping me realize that the difficulties made me better. Conversely, when I see people committed to being dissatisfied and not pivoting, it frustrates me...especially when the "people" refers to myself.

WORKSHEET 8
MY WORDS OF ENCOURAGEMENT

In your hardest moments, the words you tell yourself matter. Doubt, exhaustion, and fear can cloud your vision, but the right words can anchor you to your truth. That's why great leaders don't rely only on external motivation—they cultivate internal strength through personal affirmations and self-awareness.

This worksheet will help you create a personal arsenal of encouragements that you can call on when challenges arise. By identifying the words that have positively shaped you, crafting messages for your toughest moments, and tailoring affirmations to your weaknesses, you will build a foundation of resilience that no external challenge can shake.

- **Your Favorite Life-Changing Advice**: Write down the words that have transformed your thinking.

- **Your "Break Glass in Case of Emergency" Message**: If you could send a message to yourself on your hardest day, what would it say?

- **Personalize Encouragement for Your Weak Spots**: Identify where you struggle most—self-doubt, fear, burnout—and create affirmations that counter those moments.

These words aren't just reminders—they are weapons against doubt, lifelines in uncertainty, and proof of the strength you've already built. When fear creeps in, when setbacks shake you, these messages will guide you back to yourself.

By crafting your own words of encouragement, you take control of your mindset. You stop letting outside voices define you and start anchoring yourself in your own truth. This is how confidence is built—not by waiting for reassurance, but by creating it from within.

JOHN'S MANIFESTO EXAMPLE

Favorite Life-Changing Advice

- Be you.
- Maybe if we knew everything, we'd forgive everything too.
- Your raise becomes effective when you do.

"Break Glass in Case of Emergency" Message

- You've got this. Be you.
- You're the right man for the job.
- Challenges don't define me; they refine me.

Encouragement for Tough Moments

- A lot of people want you to be successful in this.
- You've already overcome worse. This too shall pass.
- Take a breath. Trust yourself. Move forward.

WRAP-UP

THE MANIFESTO THAT WILL CHANGE EVERYTHING

THE BE YOU! MANIFESTO™ IS NOT JUST ANOTHER LEADership tool—it's a revolutionary shift in how you approach life, leadership, and personal fulfillment. It removes the unnecessary stress, the wasted energy, and the fear-driven decision-making that holds so many people back. By mastering Core Identity, Boundaries and Relationships, and Energy Management, you become the kind of leader who doesn't just survive challenges, but thrives through them. You gain an unshakable foundation that allows you to move through life with purpose, confidence, and total alignment with who you are.

At this point, you have two choices: continue leading the way the world expects you to, making decisions to avoid being misunderstood and constantly questioning yourself...or step into the most powerful, clear, and effective version of yourself possible. The Be You! Manifesto™ gives you a road map to operate at your highest level, eliminating the stress, inefficiency, and self-doubt that plague most people.

This isn't just about leading—it's about thriving. And it can start today.

PART 3

ACT & RECOVER TOOLKIT™

OVERVIEW TO THE ACT & RECOVER TOOLKIT™

For a long time after starting Resicom, I was in charge but not in control—stretched thin by chaos, weak boundaries, and a fading sense of who I was.

For years, I dreaded working with people. Not because I didn't value them, but because I didn't know how to engage without being drained. I avoided difficult conversations, hesitated to set firm boundaries, and let concerns about how others might react keep me from doing what was truly right. I thought I was being kind. In reality, I was making things worse.

I needed to free myself to be myself. That's why I built the Act & Recover Toolkit™—a set of practical tools to lead, decide, and interact with clarity and control. The Be

You! Manifesto™ reveals who you are—stripping away noise to uncover your core. The Toolkit ensures you live it. Imagine leading with calm certainty—energized by purpose, not drained by demands.

Leadership demands more than self-awareness; it requires execution. The Manifesto helped you articulate your Core Identity and definition of a good person. The Act & Recover Toolkit™ helps you *activate* that good person in four key ways:

- **Ensuring Alignment**: Without clarity in identity, you're reacting, not leading. This Toolkit helps you reflect, cut distractions, and align actions with values daily.

- **Building Resilience and Fostering Growth**: Every leader faces setbacks. This Toolkit turns obstacles into momentum, building resilience to face challenges fearlessly.

- **Driving Clarity and Decision-Making**: Stop second-guessing. Clarity means moving forward despite uncertainty. This Toolkit cuts through the noise and drives decisive action.

- **Leading with Energy and Sustainable Leadership**: High performers don't struggle with ambition; they struggle with energy. Invest in what matters: Lead with focus and calm, ending your day energized, not exhausted.

The Be You! Manifesto™ reveals your core. This Toolkit brings it to life. It's time to step fully into yourself.

Visit *www.johnfairclough.com/book-resources* to access the Act & Recover Toolkit™ and more resources.

ACT TOOL

ACTIVATING MyOS™
A Weekly 1-on-1 with Yourself

F YOU'RE LIKE MOST OF THE LEADERS I TALK TO, YOU grind through your weeks in reaction mode—letting emails, meetings, and urgent distractions steal time from what actually matters. The result: You end up drained, off track, and wasting hours on low-value tasks, despite working twice as hard. This is true even if you're a high performer; if you are, it's likely you feel under-accomplished—not because you're slacking, but because you haven't found a way to protect your time and energy.

This tool fixes that problem. Your MyOS™ Weekly 1-on-1 is a key component to staying on track. Your energy, focus, and leadership aren't limitless resources—without deliberate recalibration, you will waste time, lose momentum, and burn out.

Why This Works, and Why You Need It

- **Eliminates wasted time**: This system saves hours every week by keeping priorities clear and aligned.

- **Reduces stress and mental fatigue**: Knowing what truly matters removes decision fatigue and prevents reactivity.

- **Builds long-term resilience**: By tracking growth and alignment, you create momentum instead of burnout.

This is your weekly check-in—your system to ensure you execute on what matters. The first few times you do this, it will challenge you. You'll map out who depends on you, who you lean on, where you're bent, and what needs focus. And once your grid is locked, you'll consistently show up as yourself and perform well.

ESTABLISHING YOUR AGENDA TOPICS

First, customize your MyOS™ agenda. There are four areas that need clarity—these will become the foundation of your weekly review. Think of this first time as a draft: Just get something down. You can edit and refine as needed.

This is a meeting from you to you—designed to help you be yourself more consistently.

Proactively doing what is properly expected of you isn't just responsible; it's honorable. It's what clears the way for true freedom. When you set clear expectations for yourself and those around you, you eliminate misunderstandings, prevent wasted time, and gain the ability to focus on what truly matters.

By defining your role in the lives of those who look up to you, those who depend on you, and those you rely on, you create an ecosystem of accountability that strengthens relationships, builds trust, and amplifies your leadership. This isn't about restriction—it's about empowering yourself and others to operate at their best.

KEY PEOPLE, PRIORITIES, AND PERSONAL DEVELOPMENT ORGANIZER

1. **People who depend on you** (team, family, clients, business partners, mentees)
   - Create a list of the core people or groups who count on you to lead, deliver, or decide.
   - Are they getting what they need from you? Are you proud of how you're showing up for them?
   - What do they need from you right now?

2. **People you depend on** (mentors, advisors, inner circle, key relationships)

- Who do you need to check in with, learn from, or gain insights from?
- Have you verified they clearly understand what you need from them (rather than simply assuming you understand)? The goal of this step is to avoid the pitfalls of assumption.
- Create a list of three to five people who keep you sharp, accountable, and supported.

3. **Work and leadership responsibilities** (high-impact projects, key goals, long-term moves)
    - What are your biggest priorities at work?
    - What major items really need your focus and execution?
    - Are you focusing on what moves the needle? Putting out too many fires?
    - Identify three to five core work responsibilities and assess your focus and execution.

4. **Long-term growth and personal development** (future-proofing your leadership and life)
    - What are you building toward beyond this week?
    - What dreams are you pursuing?
    - What habits, skills, knowledge, or resources need attention?

- Write down your long-term goals and ensure your daily actions align with them.

People often ask me how to become more successful in business. I tell them, "If you want to do excellent work, stop doing less-than-excellent work." Most people hear that as a push to work harder and improve, and yes, do more of what aligns with your standards. But just as important is pruning what drags you down. Excellence is not just effort; it is intentional focus. You have to know what to start, what to stop, and what to continue.

I remember coaching a young leader who felt stuck. She was working long hours but making no real progress. We sat down and looked at where she was trying to get to in the company. It was clear the path to more authority and pay meant growing her people, not just her tasks. The thing she disliked—dealing with underperformers—was exactly what would develop her leadership. When I told her that, she was caught completely off guard. But it struck a chord. Soon, she came to see that complaints were just noise. Once she pruned those blame sessions, she freed up time, energy, and confidence to build people up and do her best work.

Pruning what drags you down, like development, is essential to long-term advancement. Do more of what lifts you up and less of what holds you back. Your future self will thank you. Every strong branch grows stronger when you cut away the dead ones.

Once these areas of progress are established, add them to your weekly agenda.

WEEKLY AGENDA

Pick a day of the week that you'll commit to doing the following (I do mine on Sunday as I prep for the week, but whatever day works for you is fine):

1. Celebrate what's working. Take a moment to acknowledge wins before fixing problems.
   - What are you really proud of from the past week?
   - What aligned very well with your definition of a good person?

2. Address your key areas.
   - Key relationships: What did you do well? What's missing that you'd like to correct?
   - Main responsibilities: What did you execute well? Where did you get off track?
   - Long-term goals: Did you move forward on them this week? What's missing?

3. Address your Core Identity misalignment.
   - Where did you act in a way that didn't align with who you want to be?

- How would you have preferred to handle it?
- Do you need to go back and address it?

4. Where are you holding yourself to an unnecessary standard?
   - Where are you putting too much pressure on yourself or others?
   - What do you need to adjust or reset?

5. Address difficult conversations you need to have.
   - Difficult conversations build trust, clarity, and momentum. Where do you need to speak up?
   - Who do you need to check in with?
   - What difficult conversation would really help someone?

6. What difficult decisions are coming up?
   - Decisions made in chaos lead to regret.
   - Decisions made with clarity lead to impact. Schedule time to run them through the next tool: FOCUS.

7. Create your to-do list based on your answers.
   - Convert your insights into action.
   - Set due dates for each step.

ACTIVATE YOUR WEEKLY 1-ON-1

Now that you have your agenda, it's time to activate it.

- **Pick a time when you are clear-minded**—whether that's Sunday night, Monday morning, or another pocket of time when you're not in reactive mode.

- **Schedule your Weekly 1-on-1 like a real meeting.** Treat it like an appointment with your most important client—your future self.

I schedule mine like a leadership meeting—with notes, a recap, and a commitment to show up. This twenty-minute recalibration ensures you are leading your week instead of being dragged by it.

HOW RESEARCH BACKS THIS TOOL

Proactively identifying responsibilities and acting with intent ensures better decision-making, reduces stress, and increases productivity. Research consistently proves the power of structured self-reflection and prioritization:

- Locke and Latham in 2002 found that proactively identifying responsibilities and acting with intent spikes performance by 25 percent.

- Ryff and Keyes in 1995 found that taking control of your time reduces stress and increases clarity.
- Baumeister et al. in 1998 found that decision fatigue fades—you set it once, then execute.
- In 2018, Clear found the strongest leaders don't just plan—they execute consistently.

TAKEAWAYS

Your Weekly 1-on-1 isn't optional—it's essential. It's the difference between running your week with clarity and confidence, or watching it spiral into chaos.

Remember, the most successful people don't just set great strategies—they maintain them. Life moves fast, and without intention, it's easy to lose sight of who you are and what truly matters.

Lead yourself well. Keep your priorities locked in. Build the discipline that makes you indestructible.

ACT TOOL

FOCUS

Your Difficult Decision Framework

YOUR BRAIN IS WIRED TO OVERTHINK. MOST PEOPLE struggle with difficult decisions because they are pulled in multiple directions—external pressures, fear of regret, or the weight of expectations. But the best decisions come from within, rooted in personal truth rather than external influence. Making decisions that align with your core values is essential for mental health and emotional stability. When your actions reflect your beliefs, you experience reduced anxiety, increased satisfaction, and stronger relationships. When your choices reflect who you truly are, you move with certainty, free from the weight of indecision. On the other hand, decisions that contradict personal values lead to significant psychological distress.

The FOCUS framework is designed to help you systematically approach difficult decisions, ensuring they align with your deepest values and long-term vision. By following this structured method, you can transform decision-making from a source of stress into an empowering process that reinforces your identity and strengthens your leadership. It helps you make decisions you can be proud of.

THE FOCUS FRAMEWORK

- **F: Formulate the decision's essence.** Strip away distractions to identify the real issue at hand. What are you solving? Why does it matter? Write it down—clarity saves willpower.

- **O: Overlay with your core values and core virtues.** Does this decision align with your principles, or does it require compromise?

- **C: Contemplate the impact and consequences.** Consider the ripple effect of each choice. Which choices will solve problems versus creating bigger ones down the road?

- **U: Unite with wisdom and admiration.** Seek guidance from those you respect and reflect on past decisions that made you proud and how they relate to the present choice. See it as a chance to grow—what would your best self do?

- **S: Smile at your solution.** If you can't smile at your decision with peace, revisit previous steps. The right choice should reinforce your values, vision, and identity. Feel the relief—it's your gut saying yes.

WHY THIS WORKS

- **Eliminates Decision Fatigue**: This framework provides a clear structure, reducing stress and indecision.

- **Strengthens Your Leadership**: Leaders who make values-aligned choices inspire trust and consistency.

- **Reduces Anxiety**: When decisions align with who you are, you eliminate inner conflict.

- **Improves Relationships**: Clarity in decision-making fosters better communication and understanding.

- **Creates Long-Term Confidence**: Knowing your choices reflect your true self leads to peace and stability.

One time I had a really strong candidate who wanted to join our team. On paper, they had every qualification you could want. They were driven, talented, and said all the right things. But something felt off. I couldn't shake the sense that they would drain more energy than they added. Their ambition was real, but so was the tension they carried with them.

I spent time sitting with that tension. I asked myself if bringing this person on would align with who I am and what our culture stands for. Almost immediately, a clear answer emerged: It wouldn't. It would have been easier to justify the hire, focus on their strengths, and push down my concerns. But sometimes the hardest leadership decision is the one you don't make—the door you don't open.

Protect who you are, and you will always be at peace with your decisions.

HOW RESEARCH BACKS THIS TOOL

Studies have shown that aligning decisions with personal values leads to greater satisfaction and well-being:

- Sheldon and Elliot, 1999, in *Journal of Personality and Social Psychology*: Individuals who make decisions consistent with their core values experience enhanced fulfillment and reduced stress.

- Deci and Ryan, 2000, on Self-Determination Theory: Autonomy in decision-making—choosing actions that align with one's true self—fosters psychological well-being and personal growth.

- Festinger, 1957, on Cognitive Dissonance Theory: When actions contradict deeply held values, individuals experience stress and psychological discomfort, which can lead to regret or anxiety.

- Baumeister et al., 1998, in *Social Psychology Bulletin*: Decision-making based on internal clarity strengthens identity and long-term resilience, reducing impulsive or regretful choices.

Moreover, research suggests that understanding and prioritizing personal values improves relationships. When individuals are clear about their values, they communicate more effectively and establish stronger connections with others who share similar principles. This clarity reduces conflicts and fosters mutual respect, leading to more harmonious and fulfilling relationships.

ACT TOOL

SHARE YOUR GRATITUDE

Rewire Your Mind, Transform Your World

As we explored in Paradox 5, being accountable to your blessings is crucial to being a great leader. Gratitude isn't just something you feel—it's something you do. It's a practice that rewires your brain, strengthens your leadership, and shifts the way you experience life. Most people are wired to spot problems, but when you make gratitude a habit, you train yourself to see what's right, not just what's wrong.

High performers often bulldoze through life, checking off wins but missing the simplest and most powerful tool they have: appreciation. A well-placed thank-you isn't just good manners—it's a force multiplier. It strengthens bonds, builds trust, and fuels momentum. Leaders who express gratitude create environments in which people feel seen and valued, making them more engaged, motivated, and willing to go the extra mile.

This isn't about pretending everything is perfect. It's about shifting your focus from what's missing to what's working. It's about seeing people, recognizing effort, and reinforcing the kind of behavior that creates real impact. It's about choosing to be the kind of person others want to follow.

WHY GRATITUDE WORKS

- **Cuts Stress**: pulls you out of anxiety, lowering cortisol and stabilizing your mind

- **Boosts Mood**: activates dopamine and serotonin, giving you an instant mental edge

- **Strengthens Health**: lowers blood pressure, inflammation, and heart disease risk

- **Builds Trust**: makes others feel valued, increasing loyalty and engagement

- **Increases Resilience**: helps you reframe setbacks and focus on solutions

- **Sharpens Leadership**: people follow those who appreciate them, not just instruct them

- **Flips Negativity**: breaks the brain's bias for threats, opening your eyes to wins

This isn't just about feeling good—it's about leading better.

HOW TO DO IT: THE GRATITUDE PLAYBOOK

- **Daily Gratitude Hunt**: Find at least one moment every day to say thank you. Better yet, set up situations where you have to—like seeking advice or asking for help. Tie each thank-you to a routine—coffee, lunch, locking the door.

- **Write It Down**: Who did you thank? Why? How did it feel?

- **Feel It, Don't Fake It**: A shallow "thanks" doesn't cut it. When you say "thank you," take a second to really feel it. Let yourself recognize why you're grateful and let it shift your energy. Make each thank-you personal—mention the specific impact someone had.

- **One Extra Deed**: Every day, do at least one small act of kindness—no excuses. Hold a door, send a note, cover a task, make an introduction. These micro-moments build goodwill and momentum. Look for low-effort, high-impact kindness.

- **Nightcap Reflection**: Before bed, replay your day. What went right? Who helped? Thank yourself too—what did you nail today? Do one last good deed—send a message, express thanks, or set up success for someone tomorrow. You'll sleep better knowing you made a positive impact. Finally, take sixty seconds to acknowledge one moment of gratitude before bed.

- **Gratitude Letters**: Once a month, write a detailed, raw, unfiltered letter to someone who's shaped you. Share it if you can—face-to-face, on a call, or in writing. If you can't, write it anyway. Studies show this practice increases happiness for weeks—and when shared, it deepens relationships exponentially. Write a one-paragraph gratitude letter this month and deliver it.

THE EFFECT

Gratitude isn't just a mindset shift—it's a leadership transformation. When you make gratitude a habit, you:

- **Become More Resilient**: You stop fixating on problems and start recognizing opportunities.

- **Strengthen Your Team**: People work harder for leaders who appreciate them.

- **Improve Your Decision-Making**: A grateful mind is a clear mind, and a clear mind is less prone to overreacting.

- **Attract the Right People**: Positivity draws others in—people want to be around leaders who see the good in them.

- **Change the Energy in a Room**: Your presence shifts from demanding to empowering.

- **Set the Tone**: Teams mirror grateful leaders, lifting morale 30 percent per Grant's 2014 research. One act feels small, but 365 extra kindnesses a year turn into a legacy. It's not about being soft—it's about being the kind of person who makes a difference, every day.

HOW RESEARCH BACKS THIS TOOL

Psychologists call gratitude a game changer for emotional and physical resilience. Here's why:

- **Gratitude Boosts Mental Health**: Emmons and McCullough, in a 2003 *Journal of Personality and Social Psychology* article, found gratitude journaling increases happiness by 25 percent and reduces depressive symptoms.

- **Lowers Stress and Anxiety**: A *Forbes* 2014 article by Travis Bradberry shows gratitude cuts stress by 23 percent, lowering cortisol.

- **Strengthens the Heart**: Grateful people have lower blood pressure and inflammation, cutting heart disease risk, according to a 2019 UCLA Health resource.

- **Increases Resilience**: Fredrickson, in a 2004 *Emotion* article, shows gratitude broadens cognitive flexibility, speeding setback recovery.

- **Reinforces Social Bonds**: A 2004 *Journal of Personality and Social Psychology* article says gratitude boosts trust and relationship strength.

- **The Power of Gratitude Letters**: Seligman et al., in an *American Psychologist* study published in 2005, found writing and sharing gratitude letters lifts well-being for weeks.

The science is clear—gratitude isn't just a feel-good practice; it's a high-performance strategy. Commit to this, and you're not just nicer—you're tougher. Gratitude doesn't soften you; it sharpens you. Start today. Thank someone. Do something kind. Watch it ripple.

ACT TOOL

MANIFESTO LITE
(Warning Label)

YOUR BE YOU! MANIFESTO™ IS A ROBUST SUCCESS GUIDE that contains lots of personal information. To simplify communication, create a Manifesto Lite—a quick guide for you and the other person you will be interacting with. I treat it like a Warning Label for people wanting to work with me.

People work best when they know what to expect—from you and from each other. A quick guide will help ensure alignment, reduce miscommunication, and create a more effective working relationship.

To create your Manifesto Lite, reflect on the following questions. Then, write down your answers. Like all the other exercises I've shared with you, there are no right or wrong answers—as long as you're authentic to you (your core values, your Core Identity, and so on), you're doing it right.

- **What matters most?** What motivates your decisions? What are your overarching objectives?

- **What matters to your mutual organization (if applicable)?** How do your roles align with the company's success?

- **Provide your Standard Boundaries.** (From Lesson 1 of the Be You! Manifesto™.)

- **Provide advice and tips (from Insights from Others).** (From Lesson 2 of the Be You! Manifesto™.)

This simple exercise will save everyone lots of aggravation and time.

HOW TO USE YOUR WARNING LABEL IN REAL LIFE

Your Manifesto Lite isn't just for you. It is a powerful way to help people work better with you. Once you've created it, don't keep it in a drawer. Share it with your direct reports, key partners, or even your manager if it feels right. Here are a few practical ways to put it into practice:

- **Kick off one-on-ones with it.** Use it as an opener when working with a new teammate. Walk them through your Manifesto Lite, and invite them to share what matters to them too. This sets the tone for trust right away.

- **Make it mutual.** Encourage your team or peers to create their own Manifesto Lites. Swap them. It is not about rigid rules. It is about working smarter together.

- **Use it for check-ins.** Revisit your Manifesto Lites together once a quarter. Ask, "Is this still true? Are we still respecting each other's best ways of working?" It keeps alignment strong when work gets busy.

- **Address conflicts with it.** When tension pops up, go back to your Manifesto Lite. It is a tool for resetting expectations without making it personal. It helps you address problems before they fester.

Don't wait to put this into action. Draft your Manifesto Lite, pick one person you trust, and share it this week. If the relationship truly matters, put in the time: Use it as a small experiment and see what shifts.

RECOVER TOOL

RESTORE

The MyOS™ Trust & Apology Framework

Remember when we talked about taking accountability? Or how vulnerability is a superpower? Well, part of each of those things is taking ownership of all your actions—even the ones that hurt others.

To do that, you have to be willing to apologize, to step up and say, "I messed up, and I'm sorry." But here's the thing: Weak apologies—like "Sorry if you're mad" to others or "I'll just try harder" to yourself—crash your MyOS™. They dodge the wreckage, leaving anxiety, shame, and disconnection to eat away at your relationships, your credibility, and your confidence.

RESTORE is different. It's a structured, research-backed system to own your mistakes, repair trust—whether with a team, a relationship, or your own integrity—and rise stronger.

Forgiveness isn't a quick reset; it's a real process. Apologies that don't involve meaningful action don't just fail—they make things worse. RESTORE ensures that your trust-repair process is clear, is actionable, and actually rebuilds the foundation of trust instead of further eroding it.

When done right, this rewires how you handle failure, conflict, and self-respect. Instead of dreading mistakes, you become confident in your ability to own, fix, and grow from them. This is how you become psychologically indestructible.

People choke on apologies for so many reasons. They fear looking weak. They believe admitting fault will damage their credibility. Sometimes, they seek validation instead of repair. They just want to be forgiven, rather than actually fixing the damage. People also have a tendency to overthink the fallout. They delay addressing the issue, which only worsens it over time. Finally, many confuse guilt with accountability. Feeling bad about something doesn't fix it. Action does.

All of these reasons lead to half-hearted apologies, empty promises, and broken trust.

THE STEPS TO RESTORE TRUST

Instead of weak apologies, follow the RESTORE framework process:

1. **R: Recognize responsibility.** Face the fear—writing it down can be helpful. "I'm not weak for this."
   - External example: "I own missing that deadline—that's on me."
   - Self example: "I let myself down by not speaking up—I see that now."

2. **E: Express remorse.** Say it raw. No excuses, no polish—just truth.
   - External example: "I'm sorry I hurt you—that wasn't right."
   - Self example: "I'm sorry I pushed too hard—I deserve better."

3. **S: Seek understanding.** Listen before justifying. Let the truth land.
   - External example: "I hear how my mistake affected you—what else?"
   - Self example: "I felt overwhelmed—why did I let that build up?"

4. **T: Take action.** Prove it. Words mean nothing without real effort.
   - External example: "I'll cover your next task to make this right."
   - Self example: "I'll set boundaries—no more overcommitting."

5. **O: Offer consistency.** Track it. Rebuilding trust requires predictable reliability.
   - External example: "I'll check in weekly—watch me follow through."
   - Self example: "I'll stick to my plan—small wins, every day."

6. **R: Request patience.** Trust takes time to rebuild. Give it space to grow.
   - External example: "Give me time to earn this back—I will."
   - Self example: "I'll go easy on myself—it's a process."

7. **E: Earn it back.** Trust is never given freely after it's broken—it's earned.
   - External example: "I'll show up consistently until you trust me again."
   - Self example: "I'll rebuild my confidence—one step at a time."

Most apologies fail because they dodge the hard stuff. RESTORE doesn't let you skip these steps. It forces you to rebuild trust—the core reason to apologize.

HOW RESEARCH BACKS THIS TOOL

Psychological research consistently shows that genuine apologies must go beyond words. Studies highlight key factors in effective apologies:

- Lewicki, Polin, and Lount found in 2016 that taking responsibility increases forgiveness and lowers resentment.

- Scher and Darley, in 1997, found that acknowledging the impact is crucial for repairing relationships.

- In 2011, Slocum et al. discovered that commitment to change strengthens long-term trust.

- Baumeister in 1997 found that time and consistency matter—actions must align with words to rebuild credibility.

The RESTORE framework isn't just a tool for apologies—it's a tool for leadership, accountability, and growth. The people who master this process don't just fix broken trust—they create unshakable relationships built on integrity.

TAKEAWAYS

A real apology isn't just about feeling better—it's about making things right. RESTORE ensures that when you apologize, you're not just saying sorry—you're rebuilding trust, proving growth, and strengthening relationships.

Every time you skip a real apology, you weaken yourself. Every time you own, fix, and rebuild, you become stronger, more respected, and more unshakable. This is how you recover from setbacks, mend relationships, and lead with integrity. Whether it's with a colleague, a loved one, or yourself—stop running from the misstep. Face it. Fix it. Grow from it.

This isn't just about repairing trust—it's about proving who you are.

RECOVER TOOL

OPTIMIZATION MINDSET

HIGH PERFORMERS AREN'T DROWNING IN TASKS—they're optimizing for impact. Success isn't about doing more; it's about doing the right things with precision. Most people mistake busyness for productivity, filling their days with unnecessary tasks, distractions, and work that someone else could do better, faster, or cheaper. Most wear their workload like a badge of honor, mistaking endless hustle for progress, while the best optimize to stay sharp and effective.

The result? They stay stuck—overloaded, exhausted, and constantly fighting fires instead of leading with focus. This tool forces you to rethink your workload, remove inefficiencies, and empower others to drive results. It's a reboot so you can focus on what actually moves the needle. Because your impact is not how much you carry personally—it's how much you and your team carry effectively.

When you use this tool to optimize your mindset, you:

- Reduce wasted time by cutting or redesigning low-value work
- Shift from execution mode to leadership mode
- Diminish stress and urgency, and avoid unnecessary fire drills and interruptions
- Build stronger teams and multiply your impact by empowering others to step up

A key part of this is creating your To-Don't List. The To-Don't List isn't just about dropping tasks; it's about freeing your time and energy for what only you can do. Many leaders, myself included, have fallen into the trap of doing too much, confusing activity with effectiveness. The To-Don't List creates clarity by spotlighting distractions, time-wasters, and low-value habits that drain your energy and slow your team's growth.

This is about becoming more effective. Leaders who optimize don't just save time; they build a culture where everyone thrives. Empowerment turns your team into a multiplier—your focus sharpens as their ownership grows.

STEP-BY-STEP PROCESS

1. Eliminate, Automate, Delegate

Start by evaluating where your time is going. List all your recurring tasks and responsibilities. Then ask yourself:

- Would someone else be able to do this better, faster, or cheaper?
- Does this task actually move the needle on my goals?
- Is this something only I can or should be doing?
- Does this task pull me into urgent work that prevents me from focusing on important work?
- Would my team be stronger if someone else owned this responsibility?

Action One

Now, categorize each task into one of three buckets:

1. **Eliminate**: If it doesn't add real value, stop doing it. Get rid of unnecessary reports, meetings, approvals, or tasks that exist out of habit.

2. **Automate**: If it's repetitive, find a system, tool, or process to handle it for you. (Example: Automate approvals, reporting, or reminders.)

3. **Delegate**: If someone else can do it better, faster, or at a lower cost, hand it off.

   Action Two

Write down your To-Don't List.

   1. **Define Nonnegotiables**: Be crystal clear on what matters most so your team stays focused on what counts.

   2. **Encourage Accountability**: Reinforce the importance of clarity and ownership in every decision.

   3. **Focus on Results**: Evaluate actions based on whether they move you closer to your goals, not just whether they keep you busy.

2. Overcome the Mental Blocks Holding You Back from Delegating

There are a handful of common reasons why people do not delegate, and some of them expose insecurities. These insecurities often block real progress.

- **Fear of Losing Control and Wanting to Feel Valued**: "If I delegate, I might lose control over quality or people won't see my value."

- *The Fix*: Shift from "doing" to leading. Your value isn't in doing everything—it's in guiding your team to produce results at scale. Leadership is about multiplying impact, not hoarding tasks.

- **Lack of Trust in Others' Abilities**: "No one else will do this as well as I can."
    - *The Fix*: Start small. Assign a lower-risk task and provide clear instructions. Instead of expecting perfection immediately, focus on coaching and iteration. Most skills can be trained, but only if you let go.

- **Time Investment Concerns**: "Teaching someone will take too long. It's faster if I do it myself."
    - *The Fix*: Think long term. Delegating a task today prevents you from spending years doing it yourself. Every time you avoid teaching, you lock yourself into repetitive work that someone else could be handling.

- **Fear of Failed Delegation**: "What if they screw it up?"
    - *The Fix*: Set clear expectations and follow the "Delegate with Clarity and Confidence" process (below) to delegate effectively.

Mistakes are part of growth—leading means coaching through them, not avoiding them.

Action

Identify one task you struggle to delegate. Commit to training someone to take it over.

3. Delegate with Clarity and Confidence

When delegation fails, it's usually because expectations weren't clear. Use this process to make sure delegation sticks:

- **Define Success.** What does "done right" look like? When is it due? How will it be measured? What does ownership mean in this task?

- **Identify Potential Roadblocks.** What could go wrong? What tools, knowledge, or support do they need?

- **Equip for Success.** Provide training, context, and initial guidance. Set them up to own the task—not just complete it.

- **Have the Difficult Conversations.** Redefining roles can be uncomfortable, but it's crucial to address concerns up front. If necessary, reset expectations with others who are affected.

- **Make It Stick and Scale.** Check in early to correct course, then step back. Provide support, but avoid micromanaging.

Action

Choose one responsibility you will fully delegate this week. Define success, equip the person, and set a follow-up check-in.

High performers don't waste their time on the wrong things. They eliminate distractions, remove unnecessary obligations, and empower others to lead. If you constantly feel overwhelmed, you are doing too much yourself. The best leaders multiply their impact by shifting from execution to optimization. Optimization isn't doing less—it's leverage, turning focus into your ultimate edge.

Remember: The discipline to say no unlocks the freedom to lead with unshakable intent.

RESEARCH BACKS IT

Decades of research support the value that comes with eliminating low-value work, delegating effectively, and optimizing leadership impact:

- A 2017 *Harvard Business Review* article shows that people who proactively eliminate low-value tasks increase efficiency by 40 percent.

- Leaders who delegate effectively free up 33 percent more time for high-impact tasks, according to a 2018 London Business School study.

- A Gallup 2020 study found that empowered employees are 50 percent more engaged and 47 percent more productive.

- Baumeister et al. in 1998 found that decision fatigue decreases when tasks are systematized and delegated.

The fastest way to elevate your leadership is to stop doing the wrong things and start empowering the right people. Use it. Live it. Watch your impact skyrocket.

RECOVER TOOL

A PERSONAL BOARD OF ADVISORS

HIGH PERFORMERS DON'T LUCK INTO SUCCESS—THEY engineer it. Businesses rely on boards of advisors to spot gaps, sharpen focus, and weather storms. You need the same for your life. Too many driven people grind alone, betting on self-reliance, only to hit burnout, skewed decisions, or isolation. Too many people fail to recognize that strength is often a team sport.

Your inner circle isn't optional; it's your lifeline. It's a personal board of advisors—handpicked to keep you sharp, balanced, and grounded. Without it, you're navigating blind, missing angles that could save your time, energy, or sanity. With it, you've got a crew to tackle everything from soul-deep struggles to the daily hustle.

But here's the catch: Pile too much on one person, and you risk breaking what makes them valuable. Your funny friend doesn't need to be your employee—keep the roles pure, or you'll lose the recharge each brings.

Sometimes it's tough to be ourselves, and other times we lose our way. What's great is that we can build strong habits and surround ourselves with people who have our best interests at heart—people who celebrate us. Having this kind of support is valuable, especially in times of need. The Manifesto reminds us that living in alignment with who we are requires intentionality, and the people in our inner circle are one of the greatest tools to keep us on track.

WHY YOU NEED A PERSONAL BOARD OF ADVISORS

You wouldn't run a company without a board. Don't run your life without one. And don't mess it up by overloading one person—each role matters for a reason. Your personal board of advisors functions as:

- **Burnout's Antidote**: You push hard—too hard—until you're spent. A diverse circle catches you, recharging you with insight, levity, or a tough truth.

- **Blind Spot Protection**: Going it alone leaves holes—risks you don't see, potential you miss. Advisors spot what you can't, keeping your moves bold and balanced.

- **Resilience Multiplier**: Challenges don't spare anyone. A strong circle doesn't just root for you—it equips you to bounce back faster and tougher.

- **Perspective Anchor**: The grind shrinks your view. Trusted voices widen it, pulling you from the weeds to the big picture.

- **Emotional Fuel**: You're not a robot. Laughter, love, and light connections keep you human—and effective.

STRUCTURING YOUR PERSONAL BOARD

Build your board with intent. Each slot fills a unique need—internal, professional, emotional. Mix them up, and you compromise their power. Here's your lineup:

- **Internal Growth and Reflection**. Your soul-keepers, they anchor your identity and push inner growth. External wins mean nothing if you're hollow inside. These keep you rooted.
    - *Spiritual Director/Mentor*: Guides your purpose, values, and integrity. They hit you with: "Are you living your truth?"

- *Therapist/Coach*: Sharpens your mind and heart. They unpack patterns, ditch baggage, and boost clarity.

- **Professional and Strategic Guidance**. Your work war council—experts and allies driving your career forward. Vision without action is a fantasy. These help turn it into reality.
    - *Business Advisors/Mentors*: Bring industry smarts, challenge your blind spots, and see the long game.
    - *Leadership Team/Work Partners*: Your execution spine. They share the load, grind it out, and keep you effective.

- **Emotional and Personal Well-Being**. Your lifeline, these fuel your spirit and keep you sane. An empty tank pours nothing. These refill it—some with depth, others with ease.
    - *Close Family/Trusted Friends*: The no-filter crew. They know you, lift you, and call your bluff when you drift.
    - *Comedic Relief/Decompression Friends*: Not your deepest ties, but pure gold for levity. They crack jokes, lighten the load, and recharge you. Every high performer needs this escape hatch—don't turn them into workhorses.

WATCH OUT: PITFALLS THAT CAN UNDERMINE YOUR INNER CIRCLE

- **Don't overload your circle.** This point is worth repeating. In business, it's tempting to heap everything on a star performer. The same trap lurks here. If your decompression buddy—say, that hilarious friend who keeps it light—gets roped into your work grind, you'll lose the magic. Their value isn't in strategy or execution; it's in pulling you out of the intensity. Overlap roles, and you dilute their impact. A therapist isn't your business mentor. A work partner isn't your comic relief. Keep each lane clear, or you'll compromise the balance that makes this work.

- **Your inner circle must remain "yours."** Delegation is powerful, but when your leadership team or work partners make significant decisions without your input, it creates an unspoken divide. This isn't about control—it's about alignment. Without your guidance, they risk settling for "good enough" rather than pushing for extraordinary results. The best teams don't just execute; they collaborate. Keep a rhythm of check-ins where key decisions are vetted with you—not because you don't trust them, but because alignment keeps the vision sharp.

HOW TO BUILD AND USE IT

- **Take Stock**: List your current circle. Tag them—Strategic Thinkers, Detail Experts, Truth Tellers, Encouragers, Decompressors. Identify any gaps.

- **Fill the Holes**: No mentor? Hunt one. No light friend? Find that easy laugh. Balance is nonnegotiable—don't lean too hard on one soul.

- **Engage Intentionally**: Set regular rhythms—coffee with a mentor, a call with your comedian, a team check-in. Treat those moments like life maintenance.

- **Leverage the Team**: Got a challenge? Break it down—what's tripping you up? Tap the right advisor for that piece, not the whole mess.

- **Reciprocate**: Give back. A strong circle runs on mutual trust—be their rock when they need it.

RESEARCH THAT BACKS IT

Research overwhelmingly supports the power of a strong inner circle in personal and professional success. A well-structured network of advisors reduces stress, improves decision-making, and increases resilience.

- *Frontiers in Psychology*, 2021: Social support boosts resilience, cutting stress coping time by 30–40 percent for youth and adults alike.

- *Social Cognitive and Affective Neuroscience*, 2017: Quality support rewires your brain to handle stress and shields against trauma.

- *BMC Psychiatry*, 2020: A meta-analysis ties robust networks to better mental health and pressure resilience across all ages.

- American Psychological Association, 2011: Diverse ties slash burnout risk by 25 percent, boosting decisions and stability.

- *Journal of Personality and Social Psychology*, 2004: Light, positive interactions—like decompression friends—drop cortisol fast, recharging energy.

- Kahn, 1990, and *Psychological Bulletin*, 2015: Role-specific support doubles effectiveness; overlap cuts it by 20 percent.

Your personal board isn't just nice to have—it's your shield, fuel, and advantage. Build it right, keep roles distinct, and you'll lead sharper, live fuller, and rise stronger.

Overload one person, and you'll lose what makes them gold. Get it right, though, and you're not just surviving—you're indestructible.

Remember, the key to becoming the best leader (and person) you can be is to be intentional in building a life that aligns with who you are. A strong inner circle isn't just about support—it's about ensuring that when life gets tough, you have the right people in your corner to push, guide, and steady you.

RECOVER TOOL

THE BUILD METHOD
Navigate Difficult Conversations

As I've mentioned throughout this book, conflict, like failure, is often feared, but in reality, it is a necessary ingredient for growth. Managed correctly, difficult conversations can strengthen trust, deepen relationships, and lead to better outcomes. However, mishandled conflicts can breed resentment, create misunderstandings, and erode progress. The difference between these two outcomes lies in how we approach the conversation.

We've already seen that many people avoid tough discussions because they fear damaging relationships or making things worse. I was guilty of that myself for many years! But research proves that avoidance leads to deeper resentment, stress, and missed opportunities for improvement. The cost of unresolved conflict is high—teams that fail to engage in constructive dialogue suffer from lower performance, decreased trust, and higher turnover.

The BUILD Method gives you a framework to lean into tough conversations with confidence, ensuring that even the hardest discussions result in solutions instead of frustration.

Before we get into it, let me give you a quick and easy tip: Sometimes, a brief pause helps. If tempers are blazing, wait a few hours or a day to cool off—but don't let it linger beyond that. Putting it off too long will cause resentment to fester, turning a fixable situation into a full free fall of strain and distrust. The key is balance: Allow space for emotions to settle, but commit to addressing the issue before it grows into something far worse.

With that said, let's get into the BUILD Method, so you can get the mindset and tools you need to address conflict constructively, leading to stronger teams, healthier relationships, and better leadership.

THE BUILD METHOD

- B: Begin with intent. *Set a positive goal.*
  - Before starting the conversation, define the outcome you want to achieve.

- Focus on resolution, understanding, and growth rather than assigning blame.
- Shift your mindset from "winning" the argument to creating mutual clarity and progress.

- **U: Understand the context.** *Choose wisely.*
  - Pick an appropriate time and setting where both parties can engage openly and without distractions.
  - Be mindful of emotional states—don't engage when tensions are too high to allow productive discussion.
  - If emotions are running hot, take a short break—but don't avoid the conversation entirely.

- **I: Initiate with "I" statements and active listening.**
  - Use "I" statements to express your perspective without blaming the other party (e.g., "I feel unheard when my input is dismissed" rather than "You never listen to me").
  - Actively listen—reflect back what you've heard to ensure clarity and show respect.

- **L: Look for solutions.** *Collaborate and commit.*
  - Shift the focus from the problem to cocreating solutions.

- Ask, "How can we work together to resolve this?" or "What changes would improve this situation?"
- Agree on specific action steps that both parties will commit to.

- **D: Dedicate to follow up.** *Reinforce progress.*
    - Schedule a follow-up conversation to assess improvements, reinforce commitments, and address any lingering issues.
    - Acknowledge and appreciate progress to strengthen trust and reinforce accountability.

Let me give you an example of how I've used the BUILD Method. Several years ago, I was working with a company where a senior leader constantly blamed everyone else for why things weren't getting done. He would rant about how other people were not following the plan, using their failures as a shield for his own inaction. One day, I looked him straight in the eye and said, "You say you're the leader, but the truth is, you're waiting to be led." He did not see it at first. He genuinely believed he was in charge while letting other people's mistakes dictate his energy, actions, and attitude.

I reminded him that real leaders do not get led by circumstances or difficult people. They set the standard by leading themselves first. We worked through how he needed to change his behavior, not just for himself but for his whole team to have something worth following. He learned to stop excusing his drift, take ownership, and commit to his own plan instead of waiting for others to get in line. It was messy, but that shift turned avoidance into accountability. The whole team got stronger because the leader finally chose to lead, but it started with the steps in the BUILD Method.

HOW RESEARCH BACKS THIS TOOL

Decades of psychological research affirms the BUILD Method's power to turn conflict into connection. Studies show that structured, intentional approaches to tough talks cut stress, boost trust, and drive collaboration. Addressing conflict head-on with clarity and respect doesn't just solve problems—it builds resilience and loyalty, aligning with MyOS™'s core of psychological indestructibility.

- De Dreu and Weingart found, in a 2003 *Journal of Applied Psychology* article, that conflict resolution improves performance. Studies show that task-focused conflict resolution (like BUILD's intent and solutions steps) improves team performance by 20 percent when handled collaboratively.

- According to a 2003 article published in *Emotion*, Gross and John discovered that regulating emotions in conflict leads to better outcomes. Managing emotions via timing and context (BUILD's "U") reduces stress by 15 percent and enhances discussion effectiveness.

- A 1955 *Psychological Science* article by Rogers and Farson says that active listening lowers defensiveness. Using reflective listening (BUILD's "I") increases mutual understanding by 30 percent, making conflict discussions more productive.

- From *Organizational Behavior and Human Decision Processes*, Jehn found in 1997 that solution-oriented conflict strengthens relationships. Approaching conflict with a focus on solutions (BUILD's "L") boosts relationship quality and commitment by 25 percent.

- Follow-up accountability reinforces trust. Consistently checking in on progress (BUILD's "D") reduces repeated conflicts by 18 percent and builds long-term trust, per Baumeister et al. in a 1998 *Journal of Personality and Social Psychology* article.

- A 1995 *Harvard Business Review* article by Goleman says that emotional intelligence increases leadership effectiveness. Leaders who manage conflict through intent, listening, and collaboration improve their leadership effectiveness by 35 percent.

Tough conversations do not have to weaken relationships—they can fortify them. On top of that, avoiding conflict doesn't protect relationships; it erodes them. By approaching conflict with intention, structure, and mutual respect, you turn tension into trust and misalignment into momentum. The BUILD Method transforms difficult conversations into opportunities for growth, collaboration, and stronger leadership.

Ultimately, conflict isn't the problem— but how you handle it might be.

CONCLUSION

This book was never about giving you someone else's playbook. It was about handing you the tools to build your own—one aligned with the strongest, most authentic version of you.

We started with the 8 Paradoxes, challenging old ideas and showing you there is always more to the story of leadership. You learned to see the truths that others miss: that boundaries build bridges, that perfection is flawed, and that your answers to leading may never look like someone else's (nor should they).

From there, you created your Be You! Manifesto™, the clearest declaration of who you are, what you stand for, and how you will move through this world without losing yourself. Your Manifesto is more than words on a page. It is your personal operating system, a guardrail to protect your energy, your relationships, and your sense of self.

Finally, you learned about the Act & Recover Toolkit™, the practical strategies that keep you steady when life tests you. The Toolkit gives you the information you need to navigate conflict, make tough decisions, manage your energy, and recalibrate when you drift.

When you put it all together, you have something most people never find: clarity and conviction rooted in who you are, not who the world wants you to be. You have a way to lead yourself well so you can lead others well too.

When the battles come, and they always will, remember this: You are strongest when you fight as yourself.

So here's your call to action: Keep showing up for yourself. Keep fighting for alignment. Use the Paradoxes to challenge the old stories. Use your Manifesto to remind you of who you really are. Use the Toolkit to act and recover when life hits back.

You do not have to be perfect. You have to be you, fully, unapologetically, relentlessly. That is what makes you indestructible. And the world needs more of that.

Visit *www.johnfairclough.com/book-resources* to access worksheets, samples, and more.

ABOUT THE AUTHOR

If you're wondering, don't look for letters after my name, prestigious school credentials, or some guru's blueprint as the reason I was able to found and acquire meaningful businesses. The way I took a local company international wasn't tied to money or relationships passed down by my father.

I'm the son of two people whose own traumas left them unable to raise their kids. I wasn't taught how to be in business. I learned it by trying to stay mentally sound through a broken, complicated upbringing.

Let me take you back to my late teens. I was on my own, living in a car during a Chicago winter. For six months, I parked on blocks with lots of cars so I could blend in. That was my classroom. It taught me more about business, leadership, and people than any MBA ever could. The blistering cold was actually an advantage. It let me stay fully covered with a blanket without overheating. It helped me become invisible. It helped me feel safe.

I'd hear people walking their dogs, talking like life was normal. One night, a man and woman were arguing just outside my car. I stayed perfectly still, quietly planning how I would protect her if he got physical. That's what survival looked like. Quiet, alert, and ready, even when it wasn't my fight.

What put me there was the biggest rejection I had ever experienced. I had spent years bouncing to the beat of other people's drums, staying in homes that were never really mine. I could explain it away. I wasn't their son, so different rules applied. But that's not what flipped the switch. It was the rejection. The feeling of being unwanted, and worse, unworthy of help. That was the moment I started becoming myself.

My alertness was already off the charts. How could it not be, having gone to as many schools as I did? Always needing to figure out where to go, meet new people, and spot the trouble kids, because they always looked to befriend the new student. Living in the car took it even further. To this day, I don't sleep soundly when I can hear traffic. I can't sleep with a fan on because it blocks out background noise. That white noise makes me feel like danger is nearby, and I'm not ready.

Through all that chaos, I met myself.

ABOUT THE AUTHOR

I'm John Fairclough, a man on a mission to peacefully be himself and help others do the same.

It's been said that potential is a terrible thing to waste. I've willingly underperformed mine. There were seasons when I could have pushed harder or taken a bigger risk and scaled faster. I didn't. My ambition is tempered by a deep sense of responsibility to create stability. I believe that is the right combination for people who want to live a well-balanced life.

I'm also a deeply involved dad. I try not to hover, but I do offer insights I hope will make life a little more peaceful for my kids, even if it earns me an eye roll now and then. I'm more grateful for the kind of father I am than for any business success I've earned.

I created my own definition of success and a playbook to get there. Not someone else's strategy, but mine. A playbook filled with decisions that match my values, my limits, and my strengths.

I'm not here to make you more like me. I'm here to help you become so deeply yourself that no one can lead you off course. My frameworks help you trust yourself. They help you define what it means to be a good person and then live like that person.

I've battled self-doubt, perfectionism, and the fear that my real self would be rejected. I know what it's like to replay every word you said, wondering if you're enough.

So when I tell you that you can come home to yourself, I'm not selling hope. I'm offering something tested. I've proven it in the moments my life depended on it.

That's who I am. A person who knows leadership is never about power. It's about permission. Permission to be yourself. Permission to grow from your scars instead of hiding them.

Recently I was asked to have a conversation with my younger self. I guess this was supposed to be some kind of emotional exercise. For me, it wasn't. I closed my eyes and pictured myself as a young boy. I looked at him and smiled. I said, "Thank you." He looked in my direction but not at me and shrugged. I said, "You don't know it, but all those difficult things you went through helped us turn out okay. Thank you for having the courage. It was worth it." He looked back at me and gave me a small head nod. John was being John. And I was at peace.

Be you. It's the best advice anyone can give.

Made in the USA
Monee, IL
06 March 2026

45628851R00166